CALLING

All Daughters!

A Biblical Blueprint to Restore Your Mother-Daughter Relationship

Praise for *Calling All Daughters!*

"Your essential guide to rediscovering your true self through healing and honoring the relationship with your mother. This transformative book inspires you to move beyond the past and provides everything you need to create a future you once thought was impossible. With Chequita's profound wisdom, boundless love, and deep compassion illuminating your path, your journey to strengthening the bond with your mother becomes a reality."

— Erica Nitti Becker, Author of
Mastery: *The Art of Living on Purpose*

"A true masterpiece of healing! In *Calling All Daughters!*, Chequita shares her own inspiring story and her step-by-step transformational HEALING process, backed with a biblical framework for a renewed mother-daughter relationship—one that provides the needed tools to create the love, respect, and peace that you desire with your mom. If you are struggling with your mother/daughter relationship, *you must read this book!*"

— Karoleen Fober, Intuitive Business and Life Mastery Coach
and Author of *Opening to Divine Intervention:*
Expand Your Intuitive Abilities and Spiritual Connection

"As the Chief Learning Officer of Zschool and a world-renowned author and keynote speaker, I am honored to endorse this transformative book. Thank you for answering the call to be brave by picking up this book. I pray that, as a result of reading it, you will be blessed and restored to wholeness.

This profound work speaks to those of us who have faced challenges in mother-daughter relationships, impacting our self-identity and self-esteem. The author's journey from conflict to reconciliation with her mother is a testament to the power of understanding, prayer, and God's grace.

In sharing her personal stories, the author offers hope and practical tools for healing strained relationships. The HEALING journey— Reveal, Reconstruct, and Transform—guides readers to release old emotions and limiting beliefs, leading to self-love and authenticity. This book encourages daughters to honor their mothers by healing and building new, loving relationships.

I am deeply moved by the courage and wisdom in these pages. It is a powerful guide for anyone seeking to mend a broken relationship with their mother, fostering a journey toward reconciliation and wholeness. This book is a gift that will empower you to live a more authentic and impactful life."

— Dr. Sarit J. Levy, Chief Learning Officer, Zschool

World-renowned Author and Keynote Speaker

CALLING

All Daughters!

A Biblical Blueprint to Restore Your Mother-Daughter Relationship

CHEQUITA McCULLOUGH

Capucia LLC
211 Pauline Drive #513
York, PA 17402
www.capuciapublishing.com
Send questions to: support@capuciapublishing.com

Paperback ISBN: 978-1-954920-95-8
eBook ISBN: 978-1-954920-96-5
Library of Congress Control Number: 2024912476

Cover Design: Ranilo Cabo
Layout: Ranilo Cabo
Editor and Proofreader: Kevin Neece
Book Midwife: Karen Everitt

Printed in the United States of America

Capucia LLC is proud to be a part of the Tree Neutral® program. Tree Neutral offsets the number of trees consumed in the production and printing of this book by taking proactive steps such as planting trees in direct proportion to the number of trees used to print books. To learn more about Tree Neutral, please visit treeneutral.com.

Disclaimers

This book contains questions and exercises that may trigger negative emotions or experiences from your past. These exercises are intended to help provoke thoughts through the exploration of emotions and behaviors related to the past and present for coaching purposes. Issues may arise that could be very difficult to process and address. I highly recommend in these instances that you seek professional help, as I am not a licensed practitioner in the field of mental health. You may also need to seek out a professional to help you navigate the more difficult feelings and emotions around the topic of your relationship with your mother. All help is good help, so let me make it clear that there is no shame in seeking out a professional. Professional advice that can assist us in moving through the difficult areas of our lives only aids us in becoming better human beings. I would not be where I am today on my own personal journey without a licensed mental health professional. This book is merely one avenue of many for navigating your life journey.

In publishing my memories, I mean no harm to any individuals—especially my mother or any family members. While I understand others have their truth in these stories as well, I am presenting my truth as I know it.

This book is dedicated to:

God, thank you for teaching me all that I know but most importantly to "Let all that you do be done in love." (1 Corinthians 16:14, ESV)

My mother, without whom I would not be here. Thank you for all you endured as a daughter, wife, mother, grandmother, and great-grandmother. I can have the life I want because of the steps you took to pave the way. I will be forever grateful that God chose you to be my mother. I love that we were able to finally get to a place of respect and love for each other! I love you, Mom!

My father, who always made me believe I could do and be anything I wanted. Thank you for planting those beautiful seeds in my mind at a very young age. Thank you for being the other half of my DNA that makes up who I am. I am also grateful to God for choosing you to be my earthly father. I love you, Daddy!

My grandmothers and ancestors who came before me. Thank you for paving the way for my life journey.

Contents

Introduction

Hello, Daughters! Thank you for answering the call by being brave and picking up this book. I pray that, as a result of reading it, you will be blessed and restored to wholeness, with healed hearts and minds that are ready to grow.

This book is for those of us who did not have the idyllic mother-daughter relationship we wanted and, as a result, have struggled with our self-identity and self-esteem and have held back on allowing our authentic self to be front and center. Our challenging mother-daughter dynamic has impacted our ability to love ourselves and truly love others. It has impacted our attitudes toward receiving and giving love in our relationships as well as showing up powerfully in all areas of our lives.

I have written this book thinking about all the mothers and daughters who may have had a less-than-ideal relationship. I am focusing on the daughters in particular who are thinking they can never have a relationship with their mother without the tension of hurt feelings and negative words. As I share my stories with all of you, my hope is to bring awareness and understanding so that you too can come to terms with your past and rebuild a relationship with your mother that includes her in your life journey today. It is truly remarkable what God can do in the hearts and minds of people who are willing to take the first, frightening step on the path toward healing.

Never in a million years would I have expected to see myself and my mother coming to a place where I would want to be near her, hear her voice, or even be in the same room with her for more than a few minutes at a time. As a young girl from the ages of six to eight, I wanted to be just like her. I would watch her put on her makeup with precision and perfection, affix a wig on her head in the latest hairstyle, add an outfit that would complement her slim figure, and top it off with the right shoes and purse.

Even around the house, she was always put together. To me, she was bold, beautiful, and strong in presence. All I knew was that, when I grew up, I wanted to be just like her. However, sometime before I became a teenager, I lost the physical connectedness with my mother I had as a little girl. We lived under the same roof, but our interactions were distant. Where I once felt love from her, I now felt judgment and criticism. Perhaps it was because she was a stay-at-home mom for the first eight or so years of my life, so I was always in her presence. I heard a discussion between her and my dad wherein they decided that she needed to go to work to help make ends meet. Once she got that job, she seemed to disappear. She did not seem as happy as she had once been. She seemed to drift away from the warm, loving person I had once experienced, becoming a person I did not recognize or feel connected to.

As I grew, the distance between us seemed to grow as well, until one day I woke up as a judgmental teenager, which created even more distance between us. As two very strong-willed women, we spent years in conflict, seeming to never come to a place of peace on anything, never being in balance in our relationship with one another, only at odds. We continued to tear our souls apart without any tools or skill sets with which to mend and heal our broken relationship. I never saw us in a loving relationship, and our behavior toward one another demonstrated that to everyone in our family as well.

After years of struggling back and forth in our relationship, we have finally come to a place where we now interact with very little tension between us. Family members still marvel at our interactions because they cannot believe what they see. Neither one of us can take credit for this miraculous reconciliation and restoration of our relationship because we would not be here without prayer and God interceding on our behalf, changing our hearts and minds so we can see each other differently.

Life's journey is always going to be filled with triumphs and disappointments. In the case of me and my mother, we started out in triumph as mother and daughter. Then, knowingly and unknowingly, we got lost in disappointment until we successfully found our way back to reconciliation and wholeness together. Fortunately, our story will not end in regret, but was reborn with renewed love and respect for each other. I love that God gives us lots of opportunities to right the wrongs in our past. His ultimate goal for humanity is always reconciliation and restoration. Getting there takes inner reflection to reveal blind spots or defects in the old lens through which we are viewing the relationship.

Once we uncover the pitfalls and stumbling blocks keeping us stuck in the past, we can reconstruct what we want and see our futures differently. God will always bring about transformation of some sort. We are transformed individually and collectively when we can get out of our own way and out of our heads to allow our broken hearts to mend, bringing restoration to our souls. Continually living out the pain of our past only keeps us from fully experiencing the joy, peace, and love God promises to us. The reality is that none of us can go back and change the past. We can, however, change our futures to become whatever we want them to be. When I was in my 20s, a wise person said to me, "Never say never." At the time, I was in complete disagreement with that philosophy, feeling that "never" was a perfectly suitable position to take. Many years later and over time, I was proven wrong. My stance now is that anything is possible, especially with God on your side.

I am here to tell you that you can and will be able to forge a new relationship with your mother based on today, not yesterday. In this book, I share tools that helped me along my journey of reconciliation and restoration with my mother. These tools are based on the acronym HEALING. This book is designed to take you on a three-part journey of HEALING, wherein you will Reveal, Reconstruct, and Transform your soul from the inside out by releasing old emotions and limiting beliefs, and freeing up space in your heart and mind, bringing you into a space of self-love and true authenticity. This will empower you toward acceptance and forgiveness of yourself and your mother. Repairing your relationship with your mother can then lead you to live a more authentic and impactful life, building loving relationships.

The Bible tells us eight times—two in the Old Testament and six in the New Testament—to honor our father and mother. It is also the fifth of the ten commandments Moses introduced to the Israelites. As Christians, how do we honor God's command to do that when we have been hurt, sometimes to our core, by the person who gave us life? This is the question with which I have wrestled for most of my life. I have spent many years trying to find the answer, seeking to obey God's command to honor my mother. I felt like a failure in my relationship with my mother, leading to me feel like a failure and a fraud as a Christian. My distance from my mother was such that I knew I would not even be able to kiss her goodbye on her deathbed, which would lead to great regret. The mere thought of this fact filled me with anxiety. But this thought also drove me to figure out the answers I needed to rebuild our mother-daughter relationship. How could I get to a place of comfort and authenticity that would allow me to sit with my mother at the end of her life and pour out my love and gratefulness to her for bringing me into this world? This book is the process I went through to get there. It is the result of my studies in ministry and theology, as well as my experience coaching women who are dealing with self-esteem issues brought on by their experiences with their mothers.

After going through this three-part HEALING journey to Reveal, Reconstruct, and Transform with the use of the tools provided, you will be positioned to let go of past hurts and learn to love yourself for who you have become despite your past mother-daughter relationship. You will be able to live in freedom and not behind a mask, unable to let love into your life for fear of getting hurt. Most importantly, as a woman, you will be able to let love pour out toward your mother and develop the relationship that works for you today, which will honor her and fulfill God's command. Even if your mother is no longer here, there is still healing and reconciliation for you. You will be able to release the anger and regret that is in your heart toward her as you reconcile yourself to your thoughts and emotions regarding your past relationship.

I hope that, at the end of this book, your soul will be healed and restored from your past hurts regarding your relationship with your mother. I hope you will feel empowered and encouraged to start rebuilding your relationship with your mother with a new mindset, new tools, and new confidence that will bring real reconciliation and restoration to both of you in your newly formed relationship.

I am calling all daughters to invest in your soul healing and move beyond the anxiety that has been inside of you all these years when it comes to your mother. It is time to heal your soul from the inside out. Don't wait another minute or second-guess yourself. Healing the soul will be the best decision you could ever make.

Chequita
McCullough

Part 1

Journey
To Reveal

When the Spirit of truth comes, he will guide you into all the truth, for he will not speak on his own authority, but whatever he hears he will speak, and he will declare to you the things that are to come.

—John 16:13, ESV

Father,

Thank You for listening to the prayers of Your daughters over the years.

We know You love us and only want what is best for our lives.

We have come to You in need of repair from the heartbreak experienced in our past concerning our mothers.

We are grateful that You have heard our prayers, our cries, and our desires to have this area of our life restored to a place of peace.

Through this journey, we are looking forward to You revealing to us the knowledge that will support our restoration and reconciliation with our mothers.

We know that Your deep, awesome, and powerful love can help us move to a place of acceptance of the past.

In life, we sometimes do not get the experiences we want, but You in your sovereignty can take our experiences and use them to teach us things about life that help us become who You are calling us to be.

These life experiences are stepping stones on our path of self-discovery.

Through Your tender grace and mercy, we can find our healing, which will lead us to joy and peace.

As we move through the process outlined in this book, we thank You in advance for healing our broken hearts and helping us to move toward wholeness.

We thank You for helping us let go of the past and look forward with hope for the future.

We thank You for allowing us to accept that our mothers are not perfect and that we can let go of the judgment we have held onto and directed toward them.

We thank You, Lord, that You have brought us to this place where we can learn to love ourselves, let go of our past mistakes, and grow in maturity for a brighter future.

We acknowledge that none of this would be possible without You as our guiding light. Knowing that all things are possible through You helps us take the necessary steps in our individual evolution that lead our hearts to be fully knitted back to our mothers' hearts.

In this, we not only honor them but also You.

As we take our first steps to reveal what we have kept bottled up inside, we will remember to give You the honor and glory in the blessed name of Jesus Christ. Amen!

CHAPTER 1

Reveal, Reconstruct, and Transform for *HEALING*

This means that anyone who belongs to Christ has become a new person.
The old life is gone; a new life has begun!

—2 Corinthians 5:17, NLT

This book is a lifetime of lessons. I have had to learn through blood, sweat, tears, counseling, therapy, coaching, prayers, and meditation, which all led to answered prayers. I always like to ground my work with a biblical foundation of truth. But whether you follow God, Divine Love, or a Higher Self, there are life principles that are applicable to all. My intention is for everyone to come away with a good understanding of how to heal through life's journey. The world needs healing, and we all have been placed on this earth to grow and learn from one another, regardless of our belief system. I pray *everyone* is healed in some way through the journey of this book.

As you move through this book, you will learn to use many tools. The goal and intention is to help you let go of the "old life," which is your old relationship with your mother. We are going to build a "new life" with her, which is the new relationship.

2 Corinthians 5:17 tells us we get the privilege to let go of the old and walk into the new. Think about why you want to restore your relationship with your mother. This is extremely important because once you clarify your "why," you will know what you are working toward. Then imagine what you want your new relationship with your mother to look like because you are preparing to enter that new relationship with clarity and understanding.

Once I decided to focus on simply being able to sit at my mother's bedside with love in my heart and my eyes, God helped me on a journey of discovery, looking at her through His eyes. He helped me push through my anxiety, anger, shame, guilt, resentment, and hurt to get to the place I am in today. Now when I engage with my mother, I have a level of respect and love for her that works for me despite what she may say or do. Does she still trigger me? Sometimes with a capital "YES." But I now have skills and tools to help me push right past the triggered moment with love.

The three-part journey of Reveal, Reconstruct, and Transform using the acronym HEALING is the process I will use to provide you with new tools for restoration. This process is not easy, but it is necessary to reconcile and restore your relationship with your mother. This journey will be filled with fear, anxiety, tears, anger, resentment, and many other emotions. I will help you process these emotions, so you can release them and move forward. I am a master certified coach, so in this process, we will only look back to get clarity. Our focus will be on where you are today and what you need to do to move forward. If you feel there are some things you need to go deeper into regarding your past, my recommendation is to hire a licensed therapist to help you process the painful parts of your past. If you are Christian,

I recommend hiring a Christian licensed therapist if possible. They can help you process your difficult past with a scriptural context to support your growth and development. This helped me tremendously; I highly encourage it.

Each chapter of this book contains a scriptural teaching and a story of my life experiences and struggles, followed by exercises that helped me gain understanding, move to acceptance, and extend real forgiveness for my experience, which led to the healing of my soul and the building of a beautiful new relationship with my mother. I will lead you throughout the journey by championing you through the process and encouraging you along the way. After reading this book, you will have a path that is filled with reconciliation of your past experience and actionable tools to move forward in love and grace to reconnect for a new experience while building a new relationship with your mother. The chapter titles use the acronym HEALING as outlined below to provide a framework for what you can expect to go through on this journey.

- **Hard Steps**
- **Exploring the Truth**
- **Accepting the Past**
- **Letting Go**
- **Igniting Self-Love**
- **Navigating Your Healing Relationship**
- **Generational Overrides**

Each chapter represents a piece of HEALING for your broken and fractured heart. The work throughout each chapter will serve to restore each piece of the heart until the whole heart is restored. The goal is to get you to a restored heart space that will be open to receive and give love to yourself, your mother, and others. See the illustration below:

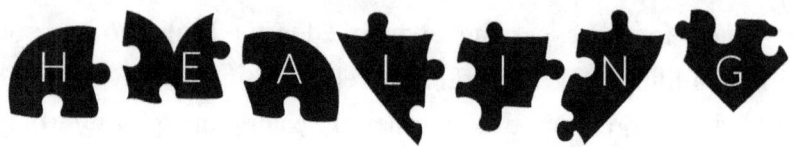

As you go through the three-part journey, allow God to Reveal, Jesus to Reconstruct, and the Holy Spirit to Transform you through the processes of HEALING.

- Reveal—You will come to understand God's perspective, especially around the importance of the role of a mother. As we move into the HEALING journey, you will take "Hard

Steps" by examining the experiences and emotions from your past and present that have formulated your relationship with your mother. You will move forward and "Explore the Truth" surrounding those emotions and experiences by examining what is behind those built stories versus the "real" truth. You will learn how these stories have been playing a part or have been showing up in your life today. Then you will explore how to "Accept the Past" that you cannot change, allowing you to move forward with a new perspective that works for you, not against you.

- Reconstruct—You will start to lay a new foundation for your relationship by learning to "Let Go" of the hurt and pain that have kept you stuck in emotional turmoil and have negatively impacted your self-esteem and all areas of your life. You will move into learning how to "Ignite Self-Love" by appreciating your journey, past and present, drawing on your new truths, and looking at your mother through a new lens. Your new perspective will support you as you "Navigate Your Healing Relationship" by bringing your mother into your HEALING journey so the two of you can start the process of true reconciliation. From there, you will work with your mother to create new familial "Generational Overrides," dismantling and breaking generational blocks, familial patterns, and limiting barriers that have held you and your family back from healing old wounds. The two of you will work together to set the future of your family on a new course for generations to come.

- Transform—You will build a new foundation by "Facilitating and Expanding God's Love" through interactions in your environment with your mother, family, work, church, and everywhere you set your feet. As you learn more about "God's Perspective on Reconciliation and Restoration," you will gain valuable tools that will allow you to gain respect, set appropriate boundaries, and learn to resolve conflict in healthy ways. By the end of this book, you will have a "Restoration Blueprint for Honor and Love" and my hope that your experience brings the "Transformative Power of Reconciliation" to your life and your relationship with your mother.

After you complete the book and exercises that Reveal, Reconstruct, and Transform, you will be able to:

- Accept and let go of the past
- Forgive and open your heart
- Heal and move forward in more love for yourself and others
- Live authentically and impactfully
- Honor and love your mother in a new relationship
- Build stronger generations to come

I want you to capture your thoughts and feelings and blueprint your future as you read this book. My recommendation is to also have a journal by your side as you read this book or download the companion guide from my website (www.chequitamccullough.com) to build your own Restoration Blueprint. We will be mapping out where you are now and then building a new blueprint for the foundation of where you are headed on this journey of reconciliation. Recording your journey is also a great way to look back and see your progress as you move forward, as well as capture moments to celebrate along the way. My prayer for you is that when you look back, you will not only see a new you but also experience a new relationship with your mother—one you never imagined was possible. I am excited for your personal journey of Revealing, Reconstructing, & Transformation for HEALING. I can't wait to read your emails about your journey of reconciliation, restoration, and love. Reach out to me via my website at www.chequitamccullough.com.

This book is not about labeling or categorizing anyone—especially a mother—in a negative light. The intention of this book is to reveal that we can create relationships with our mothers, regardless of our past relationships, through acceptance, forgiveness, healing, and love that honors God, ourselves, and our mothers. This book is designed to help heal daughters from the inside out and bridge the gap that has existed between mothers and daughters. I share stories of how my interactions with my mother negatively impacted my thoughts and feelings about myself, other people, and my own journey as a mother. Then I provide you with a system that helps you take your own journey of discovery and healing and sets you on a secure foundation from which to develop the new mother-daughter relationship your heart has desired to experience. I hope this book inspires, empowers, and energizes you for action, but more importantly, I hope it brings reconciliation and restoration of your mother-daughter relationship.

CHAPTER 2

God and Mothers

"Honor your father and mother" (this is the first commandment with a promise), "that it may go well with you and that you may live long in the land."

—Ephesians 6:2-3, ESV

Before you go into the teaching of this book, I must lay the biblical foundation from God's perspective about mothers, relationships, and families in general. These areas are extremely important to God. When you have trouble in these areas, it means there are other areas in your life that are out of sync and not flowing in the direction you would like them to be. When you come to understand these areas and their importance to God, you can start to clearly understand what your life should look like. Though you try, you cannot separate out things that are not favorable and live life in partial sections. God designed life to be lived in totality, so you must seek and find out what is not working and fix it, so you can become whole in your spirit as well as in your physical presence. You are managing two worlds—the natural and spiritual. Both must be in sync for you to get to the desired state of full love, peace, joy, and happiness.

God, Mothers, and Daughters

Let's examine the mother through God's point of view so you can gain a better perspective on the importance of the role of mothers in history. In Genesis, Chapter 3, God introduces a woman known to all of us as Eve. Adam named her Eve because she was to be "the mother of all living" (Gen. 3:20). God's plan was for the second living person created, Eve, to be the vessel who creates life for all living humans. There could be no life without Eve.

Though the Bible is filled with mothers and daughters, there is only one example of a mother and daughter interacting with each other: Jochebed and Miriam in Exodus 2. They lived in a time when Israel was enslaved by Egypt. Pharoah had given an order that all male children were to be killed to stop the growth of the nation of Israel. Jochebed was Moses' mother and Miriam was his sister. Together, this dynamic duo worked together to save baby Moses from imminent death under Egyptian law. They ensured Moses' life was spared by placing him in a basket in the Nile River. Moses was found by Pharoah's daughter and so grew up in the house of Pharoah, where he was well educated, and became a great leader. He would later use his leadership skills to lead his people out of slavery. The efforts of Jochebed and Miriam working together changed the trajectory of the nation of Israel forever. This story shows the power of the mother-daughter relationship in action, changing their family history for generations to come. This is why the mother-daughter dynamic is so important.

This relationship has the potential to change families for generations. As daughters, some of you will bear your own daughters, so it is important that you look at the impact you as a mother have on your daughters so they can grow and develop into strong women and continually lead future generations through the promises of God, authentically and powerfully.

The Challenge of Honoring Your Mother

The simple truth is there would be no life without a mother. You would not exist. For this fact alone, mothers should be honored. You should be able to honor your mother but, as you know, life is not that simple. This is especially true if your relationship has been filled with negative interactions, emotions, and words that have caused you to be hurt. This is a great challenge for many of us because our fractured experience leaves us feeling unworthy of ourselves. Our hurt and pain block us from seeing our mothers through the lens of appreciation for our very lives. Most of us need God's help to navigate the murky waters of our life experiences, caulked as they are with twists and turns. Only then can we start to feel confident in ourselves to begin the journey of discovering our mothers in a new light. What I know for sure is that God will not leave or forsake you on this journey. As you go through this book, please do not give up on the process when it gets hard. The hard parts are where the growth lies. The hard parts are where the breakthroughs live, breaking down barriers and walls, allowing new light and life in. When you stick with the process, you will get through these uncomfortable and painful parts and places, feeling empowered and self-confident with each step. While the scripture below may seem like a cliché, it is the golden nugget of your upcoming experience through this book. "And you will know the truth, and the truth will set you free." (John 8:32, NLT) Let's allow God to help set you free through truth!

God, Family, and Relationships

The next important area to look at from God's perspective is relationships. Right off the bat, we can go back to Genesis 3. He created Eve so Adam would not be alone. Theirs is the first human relationship we see in the Bible. Adam and Eve are also the first family in the Bible. Relationships are important to God, but none are more important than family. By the death of Jesus Christ, we were brought into His family and became His children, His daughters.

God hand-selected each one of us to be born through the mother He chose for us. Some of us may have been born by one mother and adopted or cared for by another mother. The point is that no matter how the relationship came to be, it is still a mother-daughter relationship. This pivotal relationship helps or hinders us well into adulthood. If it is not an idyllic relationship, then it has impacted us in many ways that have led us to places that do not serve us well. Nonetheless, it is still a family unit. Inside a family unit, relationships are formed through our interactions.

The whole point of why God sent Jesus was to bring us back into relationship with Him. There are many types of relationships—parent/child, siblings, discipleship, partnerships, ministry, community, etc. The point is that we were created to be in relationships within our families as well as with others, but familial relationships should matter most.

The Picture of Misalignment

Long before the days of social media, I could walk around displaying a false picture that my life was full and in harmony. Smiling and looking good on the outside, I was fractured and broken on the inside, pretending my life was better than it really was. In today's world, social media helps to perpetrate this lie to the point where you actually believe that what you have posted is a real representation of your life.

However, your truth cannot be made through posted pictures; it can only be made through your actual walk through life. This means your reality is often not what you are portraying to the world. Sometimes you take on self-destructive behaviors, both large and small, to make yourself feel better, but these are only temporary attempts to fix the underlying problem. Something is broken somewhere in your life. Temporary fixes can never even scratch the surface as you try to cover up the deep issues that need to be addressed in your soul. Your soul issues can only be addressed when you get serious about changing who you are from the inside out because you have this nagging internal thing pulling and tugging on your soul that something is not right.

For me, it was the negative behavior and words that showed up in expected and unexpected times. It was going against the leading of the Holy Spirit when I knew I was wrong. I often knew in my soul that I was way out of alignment with God's purpose and will for my life, but I continued on the path that I wanted, no matter the consequences to me or to others—especially my mother. I knew what I was thinking, saying, and doing where my mother was concerned was not right. The breakdown in my relationship with my mother started when I was a teenager and lasted until I was in my thirties. During this time, my soul ached and my heart felt completely shattered and broken. I thought I would never recover and become a fully functioning adult. I felt completely devastated and believed that I would never have a loving relationship with my mother, the person who gave me life. My soul cried! Scripture says, "Behold, children are a heritage from the LORD, the fruit of the womb a reward." (Psalm 127:3) I did not feel like a reward. When it came to my interactions with my mother, I felt like a target.

God's Plan to Reveal

God always has a plan for you to discover and reveal the truth for yourself. This plan is carried out over the course of your life, step by step, to reveal, reconstruct, and transform you from the inside out. Some of the lessons you figure out quickly. Some you repeat over and over until you finally get a light bulb moment that you have the power to make the necessary changes to move beyond that lesson and stop waiting on God to fix the problem. This path is filled with discovery, reconciliation, and growth for you individually, with God, and with others.

> All this is from God, who reconciled us to himself through Christ and gave us the ministry of reconciliation: that God was reconciling the world to himself in Christ, not counting people's sins against them. And he has committed to us the message of reconciliation. We are therefore Christ's ambassadors, as though God were making his appeal through us. We implore you on Christ's behalf: Be reconciled to God. God made him who had no sin to be sin for us, so that in him we might become the righteousness of God. (2 Corinthians 5:18-21, NIV)

God has given us all the "ministry of reconciliation," equipping us to reconcile our own feelings and thoughts about ourselves first, then reconciling our relationships with our mothers. When we approach this from a biblical perspective, we have a sure foundation to set us up for a successful outcome with a mended heart, capable of loving the one person we thought we would never be able to love.

As a mother myself, I had to learn how to be a mother to my son. As every mother knows, there is no instruction manual to help us get it right. We rely on many resources to help us navigate the complexities of motherhood. We also look at the ones closest to us for examples of how to be a mother. Some of those examples are very helpful, and some are not. We take on both, whether or not we realize it. This, coupled with life experiences, creates a very complex world for mothers. Some may also be managing a career, marriage, multiple children, aging parents, and their own self-discovery, which changes over time as we get older.

Many books and articles are available to support mothers in the difficulties they face every day. Without good role models, mothers are trying to figure it out as they go along. Some reach a level of success, and some do not, despite their efforts. Still others just do not care, for their own reasons.

My mother's journey started with a harsh childhood without great role models to follow. She did the best she could, considering her circumstances and upbringing. I know her heart's desire was to provide a better environment for me and my siblings to grow up in, which she did. However, some of the trauma she endured did impact us in negative ways.

My mother is an extremely beautiful woman. In Black culture, she is known as a light-skinned, or white-skinned, Black woman, which came with its own set of traumas at the time during which she grew up in Louisiana. My mother's skin is white while her heritage is Black. In her world, this led to judgments about her as a person from both Black and White people, in that she found no real acceptance of who she was from either side. She was not accepted by White people because she was Black according to the "one drop of blood" law in the state of Louisiana. She was also not accepted by the Black community and even those in her own family because she was treated more favorably than her darker-skinned relatives by the White people. She recounted the story that, when she was in her teens, one of her male friends was arrested for waving hello to her. Her father took her to the jail to prove to the White police officers that she was not White so her friend could get released from jail. In those days, Black men and boys were lynched for even looking at a White female.

This was her motivation to escape that oppression, raise a family in a better environment than the one she had experienced, and make sure her children did not have any of her childhood trauma. What she did not realize was that trauma manifests itself in many destructive ways. By the sheer proximity of coming through her womb, those seeds of trauma would be planted in us.

My siblings and I have had to reconcile with this in our own ways and learn to love her despite our experiences. When my mother looks at me now, I can see the love in her eyes that I once believed was not present. I think it was always there, but my idea of a mother's love did not match my experience of my mother's love for me.

Because of the relationship I had with my mother, I never desired to become a mother. I did not believe it was a valued position for a woman. I also did not want to have a child out of fear that my child would experience the same negative behaviors I had experienced with my mother. I did not want that experience for a child. I did not feel I was capable of loving another human being in the role of a mother.

When I became pregnant in my early twenties, I was devastated. I thought long and hard about terminating the pregnancy, but the Holy Spirit told me no. This message was so loud and clear that it reverberated in my soul. I shifted to praying that I would not have a girl baby as I did not want to have a mother-daughter tug-of-war in my future. I declared that I was going to have a boy and never uttered the word "girl" or looked at girl clothes for my entire pregnancy.

I tried to learn the baby's sex at doctor's appointments, but the ultrasounds were never clear enough. Once, when I was shopping with my mother, she asked me what I was going to do if, at birth, I had a girl. I remember getting so mad at her for asking me that question. "I'm not going to worry about that," I said. "God told me I am having a boy." I continued to look at baby clothes for a boy and never wavered.

Ultimately, I welcomed a very healthy, ten-pound baby boy into my life. He began to work on mending my broken heart and teaching me how to become a loving mother from the first time I laid eyes on him. I spent his lifetime trying to become the mother I always wanted but became the mother I was meant to be. I learned to love the mother who gave me life from a new perspective: God's loving perspective of unconditional love.

Revealing Is the Gift and Reward

First, I came to understand how God sees me, revealing me to myself. To Him, we are a reward and a gift. Then I came to understand how God loves me. Through His unconditional love, I discovered what it feels like to be loved to the core of my soul, just because. I learned that there was nothing—absolutely not one thing—that I could do to change God's love for me. None of my past actions or thoughts, or the lack of relationship I had with my mother mattered to God. He created me in His image to be loved and to love. When He reconciled me back to Himself through Jesus Christ and I accepted the reconciliation on His terms, not my own, everything changed. I began to work on myself to conform to His image and shed the pieces of myself that were stunting my growth and holding me back from fully reconciling with my mother.

Through His unconditional love, I worked through the guilt, shame, resentment, anger, and hurt I had carried in my heart and mind for all those years. The heavy burden began to lift, my light began to shine, and my love began to pour out. A healed soul has so much light and love. Each step through the journey of Reveal, Reconstruct, and Transform to HEALING brought understanding, clarity, empowerment, and action. When I worked on loving myself, I experienced real healing and became the person I was meant to become. More importantly, I gained the relationship I always wanted with my mother. The difference was my healed soul.

You cannot try to fix things when you are in broken pieces; it will not work. You must become whole in order to repair other things that are broken. It's like when Jesus said you cannot build a house on a weak foundation you have to dig down deep and lay your foundation on a rock (Luke 6:48). If you don't, the water will rise and wash away the weak, shaky foundation. When your soul is healed, it creates a solid and strong foundation that is not easily broken or shattered into pieces. It empowers you to stand up to difficult tasks, like working to reconcile with your mother.

I am now the grandmother of a granddaughter who lights up my world. Through her, I now get to experience the next-level relationship of a mother and daughter I had planted in my mind all those years ago. I can be what I wanted my mother to be for me: the "go-to person" who listens to whispered secrets and keeps them. I can be the mother figure who uplifts and encourages her through my words and loving correction. I get to lead and guide her through her own mother-daughter relationship, so she experiences love, wholeness, and self-acceptance during her most critical years before becoming a teenager. I can set her up to live life on her terms, strong and confident, by helping her claim her authentic self from the start, before life tries to move her in other directions.

It is a joy and a blessing to help her transition through life with clarity and understanding while helping her avoid as much pain and heartache as possible. I believe God is giving me a "do-over" with her, and I'll take it and make Him proud. This has become part of my calling: to build up young girls into strong, empowered young women who have great relationships with their mothers early on.

The Gift of Hope

I applaud those mothers and daughters who had great relationships through the teenage years into adulthood. I am grateful to them for being examples for the rest of us by showing us what is possible. Looking at the wonderful mother-daughter relationships of some of my friends inspired me to find this for myself. Jesus told us in Matthew 19:26 (ESV) that "with God all things are possible." Just knowing there was a slight possibility gave me the hope to find out for myself the truth of His promises, that reconciliation is possible. My intention is to get many more mother-daughter relationships to a great place, filled with love, laughter, and mutual respect. Although they are geared toward the mother-daughter dynamic, I believe the processes outlined in this book can help any type of relationship reach reconciliation and restoration.

I want to stop here for just a moment and have you visit that little girl inside of you—the one who looked up to her mother, confused by what she was experiencing that did not feel good in her heart. The one who envied other people when she saw a loving mother and daughter holding hands out in public or sharing a loving moment. Let's do a visioning exercise.

Close your eyes and connect with the little girl inside of you who had a tremendous longing in her heart to experience that kind of love from her mother. I want you to see her courage and boldness because this is the place where you knew things could be different with your mother. Take five deep breaths to release any negative energy you may have. Take more if you need them. Get to a relaxed state within your mind and physical body. Now picture a time when you were a little girl, and you did something that made you feel like Wonder Woman. Stay with this image for about a minute. Tap into her strength and belief that she could have what she longed for. Now sit with her in appreciation of what she tried to do in the past.

Now I want you to say these words to that little girl:

Thank you for all you did for me in trying to build a relationship with your mother.

Your experience was not your fault.

You do not have to hold on to the memories of your past.

You can let them go now.

You are going on a healing journey to mend your broken heart.

You have done an incredible job navigating your life's journey up to now.

It is time to move forward into your new state of being.

You can now rest knowing that you can reconnect and get to a place of love.

You are beautiful, smart, strong, resilient, and most of all, lovable.

Now take a couple of deep breaths and hug yourself. The little girl inside of you can now let go and release the hold she has had, protecting your heart from the longing for more with your mother.

A friend of mine recognized the importance of healing from her fractured mother-daughter relationship too. Her mother-daughter story is full of twists and turns, as is ours. Bre found out as a young adult that the person she called mother was in fact her adoptive mother, not her birth mother. Her adoptive family experience was not a fairy tale full of the stereotypical, loving adoption story. It was filled with verbal and emotional abuse that did damage to her image of herself.

After finding out she had been adopted and the person from whom she had experienced verbal and mental abuse was in fact not her biological mother, she realized everything she knew about herself had been a lie and that she really did not know who she was at all. She spent years spiraling out of control as a result. It wasn't until she found God that she was able to reconcile with her story and work to put her life back together again. She wanted to offer a glimmer of hope to anyone who may not believe they can be healed despite their mother-daughter relationship because the truth is we can. I hope you take inspiration from Bre's journey and her poem, which was written especially for you. Use it as inspiration as you too move through your own personal journey toward restoration, reconciliation, and love with your mother. Know that God is always with you on this journey!

Restored by God's Love
by Bre Erb

My God,

I remember when I was a little girl, tucked away in my room
I hid beneath blankets and shame.
Do you remember my pleas?
Begging you to rescue me from my family?
I do.
I remember a gaping hole in my heart,
A longing for love and safety
But my reality was fear and uncertainty.
My home was not built upon a foundation of acceptance and love
  without conditions,
Instead, it was built upon secrets,
And it slowly crumbled into a million fragments,
The burden was on me to try and keep the peace
I'd frantically sweep every piece beneath the rug
So, no one could see our abusive debris.
I remember the nights; I'd write stories in my mind of what a
  perfect mother would look like.
She'd be kind and gentle.
Nurturing and patient,
She wouldn't settle for lies or excuses
But instead push me to be confident in who I am.
She'd love me constantly, in spite of my attitude.
If I needed her, she'd be there without hesitation or obligations.
My perfect mother would freely forgive and forget my mistakes

And would never…Ever…Throw my failures in my face.
These were simple traits I longed for
And would covet another's mother whether they were fictional or
    real-life examples,
Every birthday
My wish when I'd blow out my candles
Was for a new family, A new life, and to feel safe.

It wasn't until one day,
Cancer took residence in my mother's bones
And as she slowly started to deteriorate,
I no longer saw her as the source of my pain.
But as a frail, broken woman.
In that moment,
From my eyes hurt and hate were able to separate
I could see into her heart…

She was just as hurt and fractured as me.
For years I believed everything was my fault,
And I was responsible for fixing it all.
From my repairs just like my hands,
My heart became callous.
I believed having a perfect mother,
Was the remedy, but it was just a fallacy.

My God,

When my mother was taken,
The hurt didn't go with her.

Instead, it lingered.
I searched for the answer in motherly figures,
One who fit the perfect mother image
But they still failed me.

I cried out into the heavens,
No longer from the cover of blankets and shame
But of redemption and unfiltered light.
I felt alone,
Rejected
Unwanted and neglected
But You drew near,
I released my longing for a perfect mother into Your care
And You filled it.
You are perfectly kind and gentle,
Perfectly nurturing and eternally patient,
You refute every lie and expose my excuses
Pushing me to become confident in who I am
Because I am Yours.
You love constantly in spite of me
And You are there without hesitation,
You will never leave me forsaken.
You have freely forgiven me,
And hold no record of my wrongs
But have given me a new life . . .
A new family of saints
And I finally
Feel
Safe.

You are everything the cries of my longings crave,
I was just searching in the wrong place.

My God,

You are enough.
You can fill every void lurking within us,
You bind every wound,
Fill every need
Whether it's a mother or father it makes no difference to You
Within every heart You carved a part that only You can fill,
No substance
No human
No thing, money, or degree
Could ever complete me.
May we bring our wounds to You,
Give us the desire to know Your truth
And the desperation to rest in Your Presence
May You cease our striving,
Give us the need to release all control
Soften our hearts to forgive
Allow us to see our own mother through your lens.
There is hope,
My fellow daughter and friend.
God sees you in those moments when your little heart was ignored,
He's heard every cry
The pain muffled by sobbing,
He's heard every word.
At times when pain stole your voice,

Your tears spoke to Him.
He can understand the language of your weeping.

I know it's hard to find joy in mourning
But there will come a morning
New mercies and sunlight will wake you from slumber
And you will rise in freedom.
This burden will become a banner,
A testament to our King.
He will use your story to bring another daughter hope,

So, hold on to His hand
And don't
Let
Go.

CHAPTER 3

H is for Hard Steps

Do not be anxious about anything, but in everything by prayer and
supplication with thanksgiving let your requests be made known to
God. And the peace of God, which surpasses all understanding, will
guard your hearts and your minds in Christ Jesus.

—Philippians 4:6-7, ESV

As you take a few hard steps backward to reflect on some of the difficult moments with your mother that shaped your beliefs about yourself, you cannot help but think about it with dread, anxiety, and waves of emotions running through your brain, speeding up your heartbeat, and feeling like a pit in your stomach. These are some of the moments you might not have spoken about since they happened all those years ago. You have tried to bury the experience along with the emotions, hoping to forget they even took place.

While that might sound good in theory, the reality is that these experiences have been with you along the way. Unless you have sought professional counseling to deal with these emotions, they may continue to surface whenever something triggers them, most likely in conversations with your mother. Whenever you are faced with challenging experiences or conversations that don't feel safe, you are hit with waves of emotions like dread, fear, anxiety, nausea, and even paralyzing thoughts. These emotions are triggered to help you protect yourself from harmful things like physical harm, harsh words, or the silent killers of your soul: looks of disapproval and cold shoulders when you have done something that did not meet your mother's expectations.

Nonetheless, you cannot get to a place of acceptance, forgiveness, or love without taking some hard steps on your journey of life. Most of the hard steps have already been taken; they are how you have come to this point. However, to heal, you must walk through a few more hard steps.

The good news is that this time, you will not be alone as you march down that road toward healing. God is always with you, as the scripture above tells you. He has always been there for us. In our pain, we may not have been able to feel His presence or hear His voice. However, as we move into the space that opens us up for healing, He is waiting for us with open arms. He is ready to take away your anxiety and bring you peace. It is the kind of peace that you will not understand until you arrive at the place of peace.

During this last leg of your journey where you will be releasing the memories connected to your hurt and pain, avoiding the hard steps is not an option. All the years you have avoided the discomfort, it still showed up in your life in many not-so-positive ways. It is beyond time to stop letting your buried emotions cripple you on your life journey, creating barriers in your heart and mind and limiting you from living the beautiful, authentic life God wants you to experience. People in your life—your sisters, brothers, fathers, spouses, significant others, children, grandchildren, friends, and even strangers, are waiting to experience your authentic being. It is time to let your inner soul come to full life and meet the world.

Take a moment, close your eyes, and take a deep breath. Now imagine what your life is going to be like living with a healed soul as your most authentic self. Can you feel it? Feel your heart beating in gratitude. Imagine your mind not replaying any of those old stories or flashbacks. See yourself receiving love and giving love back from your full self. Can you sense what this is like in your body? Can you see it? I can and have for quite a while now, and I am going to help you get to this place as well.

My Hard Steps From the Past

One of my most painful memories from my teenage years is my mother threatening to harm my face in some way. She never did, but there was always a veiled threat that seemed real, even though I believed in my heart that she would not follow through. I feared this could come to pass in part because my maternal grandmother's cheeks were both scarred. As a young girl, I was afraid of my grandmother because both of her cheeks looked as though someone had tried to peel all of the skin away, leaving two big circles of pink skin exposed. It looked as if someone got carried away with a blush brush and covered her entire cheeks with the wrong color blush in a circle against her brown skin like you might see on a clown's face.

I was never really told what happened to my grandmother's face. Different stories from my mother and her siblings about this condition were told and glossed over or kept as a silent secret. None of their stories ever matched. All I remember is that my grandmother was not very affectionate, so I connected the lack of affection to her scarred face. Back in those days, children were not told anything, especially in a Black family. There were always many secrets and lies around situations, even situations you saw with your own eyes. A story would be told that would contradict what you saw, but this was the story you were told, and it was made out to be true. These secrets and lies have damaging effects that, over time, appear in your mental state in unexplained ways and ultimately hurt you in your soul. Secrets and lies are the soul killers in the hearts and minds of young girls more than we can know.

When my mother would threaten to harm my face, all I could think about were my grandmother's discolored cheeks and that they could be my facial demise. If I had those facial wounds, then no one would love me. I am sure my mother had her own trauma around the color of her skin and how she viewed herself internally, which may have played a part in her focus on this area with me. Maybe the threats she hurled at me were previously made to her. I don't know; we have never spoken about why she felt the need to threaten to change the visual appearance of my face throughout my teenage years. I was called "cute," "pretty," and "beautiful" by others. I was 5'10" with a slender, athletic body, and most adults saw me as a full-grown adult—especially men, which did not help or support building a positive perception of myself as an underage child, but that is another story.

All I know is that my physical stature and appearance seemed to send my mother off into shouting tirades that ultimately ended with a threat to harm my face. This resulted in me praying to God to physically change my face so I would not have to endure the pain of the threats—the pain of thinking that my own mother wanted to take my pretty face and turn it into an ugly spectacle for others to look at and mock for the rest of my life. This was a huge blow to my self-esteem and how I looked at myself. I started to see myself as ugly because I believed I must be if this was how my own mother was treating me. This ugliness I felt inside manifested outwardly in how I interacted with people, both male and female, and even my sister. It ultimately manifested in me never feeling that I was good enough for anything. No matter how many A's I got or how good I was in school or sports, nothing I ever did seemed to be good enough in her eyes. Therefore, I was not good enough.

Grown in Love with Myself

It has taken me many years to appreciate and love the face I see in the mirror today. I always thought my face was a problem, but the truth was it was not my face that was the problem, but the false beliefs I had absorbed from my mother's threats. The untruth I told myself was that I was not worthy of a pretty face because of the negative attention my mother had given to it in my formative years. To this day, I do not remember ever hearing my mother tell me I was pretty.

She now tells me she is proud of me, which took decades for me to hear. But I have never heard words from my mother like "You have a very beautiful personality," or "You are a pretty woman." She has told other people that she feels this way, but never me. That used to bother me, but as I grew and matured, I came to realize that sometimes people who are close to us do not know how to express their feelings toward us in positive ways because they never learned how. It does not mean they do not have positive feelings; it just means they do not know how to express them without feeling some type of guilt or shame.

I look like my father and always prayed to stay that way. Then one day as I looked in the mirror, I saw my mother in my face. It freaked me out! To me, that moment meant that I was becoming my mother, and that was the last thing on this earth I ever wanted to do. I had spent years in my adult life making sure that did not happen, or so I believed, which was a lie. The nastiness and meanness of my mother's words had become part of me, and I learned to use words to cut down people's feelings about themselves like a machete cutting down sugar cane stalks, sharp and swift, cutting right through the core. This was a product of what was manifested in me through my teenage experience as I watched my mother and her sisters display this behavior with everyone they encountered, man, woman, or child.

As a young woman, I realized this was a learned behavior that my mother and her sisters had picked up from seeing the women in their lives behave this way. The apple doesn't fall far from the tree, right? This was a pivotal point for me. I could continue to go down the road of following in the footsteps of my mother and my aunts, or I could try to start walking on my own path. I chose the latter.

The Blessing of Role Models

How would I do this? After all, I did not have any role models in my life showing me a different path. Or did I? I had always been drawn to other people's mothers growing up. The grass on the other side of the fence always seems to be greener. If you look, you can always find positive images of what you are seeking. I think this is God's way of showing us what is possible for us before we get to the place where we can understand and receive it. Whether they were the mothers of my friends or older co-workers, there were always many women around to help me forge my own path throughout my life. Although I never shared my experience about my mother with them, they could see for themselves where my needs were in the way I interacted with them and the wise counsel and corrections I needed to do better and learn to believe in myself.

God is always placing the right people into your life to help you learn what you need to know—just like many of you reading this book right now. You have been searching for someone who knows exactly how you feel, deep on the inside. I recognize the patterns you have adopted in your life. You feel completely alone, even though you are surrounded by people. Maybe you are hiding from the world because you believe being invisible will protect you from further hurt. I want you to know I can see you. I know how you feel in the core of your being. But don't forget that God sees you too and knows your hurts. With Him, you are never alone. Don't ever forget that we are *never* alone. The only way I could take these hard steps was to go back to the One I knew loved me, and that is God. The only way I could change how I thought about myself was to take the hard steps toward exploring the truth of my situation.

Looking Through Spiritual Eyes

I can't go back and change anything in my past, but I can change how I look at it and how it makes me feel. Those are two things I can control. I started by praying and asking God to help me see my mother as He saw her. "If You can see her loving and beautiful side, help me to see it too, even though I'm looking through the tear-stained eyes I have been looking through all these years, help me see the love I have searched for most of my life. Help me see her love for me as her firstborn daughter. Then after I have seen this, help me replace the emptiness in my heart where I took my love for her away and replace it with a new love from a new view about her, and heal the hole in my heart."

God did just that. He showed me things about my mother I had never seen. He showed me that she did love me and why it was so hard for her to express that love to me and other people. He showed me how to extend her grace, even when I did not want to. The beauty of God's work is He showed me all of this through me, not my mother. We are byproducts of our environment, so we do not need to go to the original source of our pain. We have created enough of our own pain that we have enough examples to work through. These in turn help us cope with and handle the pain caused by our mothers to us.

Did I engage my mother through my healing process? Yes, but not from a place of judgment. Instead, I engaged her from a place of curiosity and grace. I chose curiosity simply because it felt safer than cutting straight to the chase. The truth is I was simply too afraid to go straight on and direct in my approach. Remember, I wasn't trying to drive a deeper wedge; I was trying to remove the many wedges, rivers, and valleys that already existed in our relationship. Getting even a drop of success in the hard steps would take a new strategy and approach to obtaining the information I needed. The other path had proven to be a road too volatile to travel again. God is always working on us as individuals, so it seemed logical to start with the face I saw in the mirror that reflected my mother. I had to know why I saw her face instead of my father's—or mine, for that matter.

It's time to go to the Restoration Blueprint for your first written exercise. Remember the prayer to reveal that started you off in Part 1? It is time to add on to that prayer. You will also begin to reflect on some deeper questions that are going to draw out some truths for the next chapter, "Exploring the Truth." For the prayer/reflection, you are going to ask God, Higher Power, the Infinite to show you how He sees your mother. Then you are going to ask Him to reveal *all* the parts and places where your mother is showing up in you. I want these two components added to your morning and evening prayer/ meditation/reflection time. Have your journal or companion guide next to you so that you can start to capture what gets revealed to you in prayer/silent reflection time. One thing to note is that sometimes when things come up, we want to quickly dismiss them. I am going to ask that you not be quick to dismiss what is revealed but instead simply take note and jot it down. It may become clearer to you in the future.

Now I want you to answer these questions for the Restoration Blueprint Exercise:

1. Describe in three words your relationship with your mother growing up.

2. Describe in three words your feelings about your relationship and how these feelings manifested in your thoughts and feelings about yourself.

3. Explore how the feelings you have about yourself manifest in your relationships with others. This can include siblings, significant others, children, father, and friends.

4. Think about how the parts of your mother that have hurt you are showing up in you when you are frustrated, hurt, overwhelmed, or stressed out.

5. Explore how these parts of your mother in you impact people you encounter.

6. Describe what your relationship with your mother is like today.
    - What, if anything, has changed?
    - Are you speaking or not?
    - What are your interactions and engagements like when you are together?
    - Can others feel the tension between the two of you?

7. Ask yourself where you would like the relationship to be. Be honest and answer this one from your heart, not your head.

Until you heal wounds of your past, you will continue to bleed.
—Iyanla Vanzant

CHAPTER 4

E is for Exploring the Truth

And you will know the truth, and the truth will set you free.
                                                —John 8:32, NLT

When you have unresolved issues, exploring the truth seems like a very scary place. For years, I pushed unresolved feelings down in my soul, hoping they would be forgotten in time. If you are like me, conjuring up those old feelings only leads you to a place you do not want to go. The truth is that hurts are never forgotten. They can rise up at the most inopportune times due to our unconscious and conscious emotional triggers. In this chapter, you will focus on how your experiences with your mother trigger your emotional states and how these emotions impact your actions or inaction. You will discover how those triggering moments manifest outwardly in your life. Then you will start to do some work to discover how you can stop these triggered emotions from creating situations that do not allow you to take full control of your emotions and show up as your best self.

An Emotional Rollercoaster

This book was a major trigger of emotions for me for many reasons. The process of telling some of my most painful moments publicly, putting some of my most private moments out into the universe, was and is extremely vulnerable. At the end of the day, it came down to one simple thing: If I can help one person come through their situation much stronger on the other side, then it would be well worth the scrutiny and judgment I might face from the public.

I was also worried about what my mother would think, not wanting to hurt her, because two wrongs do not make a right. In fact, I delayed telling my mother I was writing this book until I had completed the manuscript because I was in fear of how she might react. After all, I am not only telling my story but exposing some of hers too. I rehearsed what I would say many times. Finally, when I got the courage to tell her, she agreed that if it could help another mother and daughter heal and grow their relationship, then it would be worth it. When she said these words to me, I almost fell off my couch. I instantly felt relief, but more importantly, deeper love for my mother. I could see she also understood the importance of our story and how it could help others. I chuckle now, but at the time, I did not believe that we would agree on something this big and vulnerable. My old emotional triggers regarding sharing private things with my mother rose up and took over. This is an example of just how easily it can still happen.

I believe in my core that my mission is to help heal as many mother/daughter relationships through this book as possible, so the greater cause outweighs my personal discomfort. As Christ-followers, we also learn that when you get an assignment, it is not negotiable. When the thought of writing this book entered my spirit, I had a Jesus moment and asked God if this particular cup could pass me by. Although I did not hear the word "no" that I was waiting for, the reactions I got from women and men that I told I was writing a book on this topic were the confirmation I needed to forge ahead. Most people, myself included, got goosebumps. If that isn't a sign, I do not know what is. One of my spiritual sisters on this writing journey, upon hearing the topic, gave me a long list of compelling reasons why I needed to fight through my fear to put this book out. After our Zoom call, I sat at my desk and cried for fifteen minutes. At the end of that cry, I said to God, "There is a reason you picked me to write this book. Please help me make it become what it needs to be to help mothers and daughters." So, daughters, it's time to discover your truths. Are you ready to discover the truth that will set you free as John 8:32 tells us? Come on, let's go. We can do this together!

Accepting Grace Is for Me Too

Exploring the truth requires a tremendous amount of grace for yourself and for your mother. In fact, you cannot move to acceptance of the past without grace; it is just not possible. Without grace, you continue to harbor the same feelings you always had when you think about your mother, which is an old frame of reference. Showing yourself grace also increases your self-love. When you learn to love yourself fully, you can also start to extend love to others because you have become love within yourself. The evolution of self-love is critical to your healing process. When you walk and grow in self-love, you can see the truth more clearly for yourself. You become willing to see the real truth about yourself and your life without judgment. You become prepared to make real and lasting changes in new directions that support how you want to be. You become truly authentic within yourself.

One very important thing to note here is that your truth and your mother's truth may never line up. You are not looking for them to line up. But if they do, what a great starting point that will be for future conversations. The point of this chapter is to help you discover your real truth, not a truth that has been wrapped up in the story you have built and have been telling yourself for years. You are looking for the truth of how you feel in your bruised soul, what you believe in your head and heart about yourself, and what is the truth about yourself today. But let's go back and discuss grace for a moment.

Grace is really about forgiveness of yourself and not holding onto the things you did in your past that did not represent you well. God gives a fresh, new grace every morning. I like to say He wipes my slate clean every day and gives me a do-over to do better than I did the day before. Acts 20:32 teaches us that God gives us His word of grace to build us up, for which I am very grateful. When you apply grace toward yourself, you also build yourself up in your positive beliefs about yourself. The more grace you show toward yourself, the more you start to see that you are not what your mother may have told you that always went against what you believed in your heart about yourself. With each step of grace, you give to yourself and your mother, you begin to fill your souls with the full measure of grace Christ gives to you. You become full of Christ when you learn to extend grace, especially to those who hurt you. Grace will free you from the inside out to love—and love powerfully.

Separating Truth From Fiction

I also took a hard examination of my behavior and actions that contributed to my conflict with my mother. What was contributing to the fear, anger, and resentment I felt and hurled toward my mother for decades? There were many avenues I took to uncover the truth. My clarity journey started in coaching school. The program I took was developed for us to experience what our future clients would experience. Every process and step I learned had to be done through my own personal experience. I was essentially my first client. Three key things I learned in this program were where my mindset was, how I was showing up energetically—or, simply put, how my actions were impacting others—and whether I was playing the role of a victim or an empowered person in relationships, decision-making, and life challenges. Learning that I was firmly planted in victimhood was an eye-opening experience. The second thing I learned in this program was how my physical energy was showing up in the world. When you are in victimhood, you do not think anything will work for you, no matter what it may be. You live your life through a lens of negativity. Even when you have positive things happen to you, you believe they are a fluke or just a lucky moment. This coaching program was transformational and is the reason I am a coach today. People need to understand where they are and how to shift and transform into who they want to be.

Therapists and the Spirit of God

I also sought professional help from a licensed Christian therapist to ensure I would also be held accountable to my Christian values through this journey. I knew that, in order to move forward, I would have to look at the past and deal with the pain I held onto deep inside, then look at the path forward through Christian principles of forgiveness, grace, and love. Once my therapist and I developed a trusting relationship, she introduced me to a technique called brainspotting, which can only be performed by a trained, licensed practitioner. According to developer and trainer David Grand, PhD, "Brainspotting is a powerful, focused treatment method that works by identifying, processing and releasing core neurophysiological sources of emotional/body pain, trauma, dissociation, and a variety of other challenging symptoms" (Grand 2017). This was a big step for me because I felt like I was going against my Christian faith by seeking out answers from the deepest parts of my brain. In the world of church, tapping into something that is not written about in the Bible is often frowned upon. But doesn't God just want His people to be healed and whole by whatever means necessary?

Lastly, I dug deep into the Bible looking for the verses about how I was supposed to show up in the world as a Christian and started to embody the principles of a renewed mindset—love, compassion, empathy, forgiveness, reconciliation, and unity. I read and studied these principles not only in the Bible but outside of the Bible as well, such as in the mind-renewing books of Dr. Caroline Leaf, a neuroscientist who cleverly marries neuroscience with the Word of God, along with many other books about changing my mindset. I did this until I understood what it really means to implement these truths in my life. Along the way, I was praying, using guided meditation, sitting in silence to hear my inner voice, and dreaming about the possibilities of this relationship being different. Putting my real feelings and thoughts down on paper was so empowering for me. Expressing my real truth outwardly helped me allow my authentic self to come out of hiding. These were among the many daily practices that helped me transform my thoughts, emotions, and actions toward others, especially my mother. When I discovered the truth for myself, then and only then could I start the process of reconciliation with my mother.

Getting to the Core of Reality

At the core of all the issues with my mother, I did not trust that she would protect me emotionally. As a dreamy-eyed eight-year-old, I painted a picture of what my mother should be—this beautiful woman protecting her child at all costs. I am not saying my mother did not protect me, but there are two types of protection as a mother—physical and emotional. Physical protection is when she will throw herself in harm's way to protect her child, putting herself at risk. Then there is emotional protection where a mother is conscious of words and gestures that can have a negative impact on a child and is mindful to feed that child with words that build them up on the inside so they can come to believe in themself. I grew up in the era when whooping your child was considered a parent's right. However, I was not the kind of child who got into a lot of trouble because, quite frankly, I did not want to feel the physical pain of a whooping. This left my lack of emotional protection to be exploited.

As a child, I was extremely sensitive and shy. I would cry at the slightest thing, whether it happened to me or someone else. I would cry at the emotional moments on TV in commercials, movies, and TV shows, and I still do to this day. I knew I could never grow up to be a doctor because I felt others' pain in my physical body. This was highly ridiculed, forcing me to swallow my tears on many occasions. I did this so much through my teenage years that I literally did not cry for years. I physically could not shed a tear. This inability to cry came out in the form of anger as a young adult.

Due to my extreme shyness, I turned to books. My preference was to hide in my room and bury myself in books, reading for hours with little to no social engagement. My mother would send me outside to play with the other kids, but all I wanted to do was read. I used to get punished by my mother for simply reading a book. As a teenager, my deeply sensitive nature turned into extreme anxiety, especially around adults and large crowds of people. When placed in these situations, I would sweat profusely, shake, and become extremely nauseated. Fear and anxiety are a deadly cocktail when you are forming into a young adult. This deep-seated fear followed me into my adulthood and lasted for decades.

What I clearly needed was therapeutic help but, in those days, going to a therapist was not something that was considered, especially not in a Black family. The last key ingredient in the recipe for my poor self-esteem was added when my mother would tell my most private moments to all of her friends and relatives. Today, news can travel via a group text, but back in the day, my mother would start calling all her friends and our relatives, sharing my most private moments with anyone who would listen. At age 14, when I got my period for the first time, I came home from school to find her on the phone with one of my aunts, sharing my news. The phone calls went on for hours, one after another, all discussing my humiliation of getting my period at school and panicking as a result.

I learned in that moment that I would never have my mother as my best friend. I learned that she would never be the keeper of my private thoughts and crucial life moments. If I got hurt by a future boyfriend, she would not be the one who would help me walk through a bad breakup. I was all alone, without a confidant. From that point forward and even to this day, I have kept my private affairs to myself. I'm sharing private thoughts and feelings now in this book in hopes of helping someone move forward in their life.

The emotional scars I carried deep in my soul for so long manifested as anger, resentment, and unworthiness, seeping out at times through my pores like bad perfume. The emotional odor would repel people who were trying to get close to me, trying to love me, or simply trying to be a friend. When you grow up with emotional deficits, there are many holes in your soul that you cannot fix by yourself. You need help, professionally and spiritually.

Beginning to Heal Through Processes

God comes into play by helping you process those emotions that are affecting you spiritually. A therapist comes into play to help you process those emotions that are affecting you mentally and physically. Both are necessary to help plug those holes and restore your soul from the inside out. Both are needed to help you sift through to find the truth so you can move forward on a path that supports where you are trying to go.

Facing the truth can be one of the hardest things we do. When you can face the truth, you can start to move forward toward acceptance much more easily. This will be covered in the next chapter. Before we go there, I want to walk through how to get to your internal truth about this relationship. In the chapter "Hard Steps," there were some questions regarding your relationship with your mother and the feelings and emotions that have transpired from this relationship. Now it is time to go deeper inside of you to find out how you are really feeling on the inside. The goal here is to pull out your negative internal dialogue—those negative words you have been speaking to yourself, both consciously and unconsciously. Those words have been locked inside to avoid the pain and discomfort they cause you. In order to move forward and release them, you have to dig them up by their unsavory roots so they can be fully discarded. These are the words and statements that have kept you from self-love, shot holes in your belief in yourself, and caused you to hide yourself from the world around you. These are the lies you have planted in your mind to support some of the things you probably heard from your mother.

You know the statements:
I am not good enough.
I can't because . . .
I'll never be . . .
No one will ever want me . . .
I'm such a . . .
It's too difficult . . .
I have no power to change anything.
Others are just better than me.
I'm so stupid.
I wish I had never been born.
I hate myself.
I am ugly.

These are just a few of the negative self-talk statements you may have uttered to yourself about different parts of your life and your physical being. These statements are coming from a place that has been deeply hurt in your soul by your mother. These statements keep you in your victimhood, chained to the belief that you do not have any control over your life or your circumstances, which could not be farther from the truth. I completely understand how you feel here because I have said most, if not all, of these kinds of statements to myself throughout my life. However, after working with my therapist, with coaches, and in prayer and meditation, I discovered that none of these statements were actually true.

Once I came to this realization, I was able to break the bond with victimhood permanently. They were merely statements I had adopted, taken on, or made truth through my false belief that they were true. You are going to spend some time working on your Restoration Blueprint by journaling and meditating to uncover these untruths that are both out in the open and hidden inside of us. You will use some prompting questions to open up your mind and your heart to uncover your truth. Then you will do some mindset work so that your beliefs can shift to the real truth of who you are—a uniquely wonderful woman who has a bright future in front of her full of love, happiness, joy, peace, and even possibly a healed relationship with her mother.

Proverbs 18:21 (ESV) says, "Death and life are in the power of the tongue." I like to say our thought life also contains this power. What you say and think matters because what you say and think becomes the truth. The question is: which side of the truth do you want to have in your life—the side that is really true or the side where the truth is built on lies? You are trying to heal your soul, so I know you will choose the side that brings you life and not death.

It's time to go to work on your Restoration Blueprint. Go to a place that is quiet and brings you peace where you won't be distracted or disturbed. It can be a prayer room, a favorite chair, a spot out in nature, or anywhere you choose. If you are able to add some candles and soft spa music, go for it; it only makes the space more relaxing as you allow your thoughts to flow out. Have your journals, journal app, companion guide, or a roll of toilet paper to flush the truth out, or whatever you need to capture everything that comes up and out for you. Also, bring some tissues or that roll of toilet paper because you will more than likely need it. Tears are always welcome throughout this journey. Tears are so useful in helping us heal our souls. There is nothing like a good cry to release energy, both mentally and physically, so let those tears rain down as you move from darkness to light, removing all the unwanted untruths. It's time to pull up all the negative thoughts and words and release them from your soul. It's time to release death and bring life into your soul. Now that you are set in your space, I have a prayer for you. Please feel free to add words or thoughts to it to help you through this process. Just know that on the other side of this lesson, you will be creating truth statements for your journey forward. I'll see you in a little bit.

Prayer to Reveal

Father God,

Today your daughters are facing their truths head on.

Please cover them in Your everlasting love, grace, and mercy as they begin the process of unseating the untruths and planting seeds of truth as they move toward acceptance.

Show them they have no reason to feel guilt or shame about their relationships with their mothers.

Show them that restoration of their souls is possible, as is a relationship with their mothers. Your Word is full of truth, and it tells us that all things are possible with You.

Give them the measure of faith as the small mustard seed to be able to see this for themselves.

Lastly, help them to see how You have beautifully sculpted and crafted them into Your image, which is love, joy, peace, patience, kindness, goodness, and faithfulness.

Lord, on behalf of your daughters, I ask You to allow them to experience the fullness of Your love and forgiveness so they can forgive themselves for any thoughts, emotions, or actions that may not have represented You or them in the best light.

Thank you, Father God, for always hearing our cries and capturing our tears in Your sacred bottle.

In the precious name of Jesus Christ. Amen.

Restoration Blueprint Exercise
Emotional Prompting Questions

1. What thoughts or emotions come up for you often when you think about your mother?

2. Which emotions do you find the hardest to accept when you think about your relationship with your mother?

3. In the previous chapter, you found three words that described how your feelings manifested in your thoughts about yourself. Now I want you to look at how those emotions really shaped your view about yourself. What is your belief about your capabilities and possibilities as a woman?

4. What are three or more self-defeating or self-sabotaging beliefs that you have?

5. Now take those self-defeating or self-sabotaging beliefs and reframe them from the place of truth you know deep inside about yourself that is positive and encouraging.

6. What is one thing you are willing to do to see yourself through the eyes of grace in a positive light every day going forward?

7. What will it take for you to trust and let go of your past experiences?

Now that you have finished, take a moment to take some deep breaths. Exploring your truth in that level of detail can be an emotional rollercoaster, and I am so proud of you for pushing past your fear of dealing with painful thoughts and emotions. You should be very proud of yourself, not only for completing the exercise but, more importantly, for rising to the occasion for your soul healing. This is a critical step in the right direction.

I hope this exercise went well and that God surprised you beyond your expectations. How do you feel now? Relieved? Lighter? Enlightened? Empowered? Excited by the possibilities that lie ahead? Having a healed soul is the reason I now have a better relationship with my mother that honors her. This was only made possible by building and nurturing my relationship with God and talking openly and honestly with my therapist, confronting all my fears. All of it was hard. It was the hardest thing I ever had to do but it was necessary to bring me to the place I am today. This is where I want you to be too. I'm so excited for your journey forward.

Restoration Blueprint Exercise
Statements of Truth

Now it's time to start reframing and building your statements of truth for the Restoration Blueprint Exercise. Take out your journals, companion guides, etc., for this exercise. I have listed some common statements of truth I have compiled based on my experience through this journey. Below is an example of the format I want you to use to do the same for yourself. Please feel free to create however many statements of truth you like. There are no limits to the truth.

- The truth is I was hurt deeply, sometimes physically, sometimes mentally, and sometimes both.
- Another truth is my experience might not match my mother's recollection.
- Another truth is I can still be restored to a place of wholeness.
- Another truth is I do not have to let an old hurt control my thoughts, emotions, and actions.
- Another truth is I can heal my broken heart and rebuild my self-esteem, my feelings of worthiness, and the positive ways in which I see myself.
- Another truth is my hurts did not kill me because I am still here.
- Another truth is I can still make a positive impact on my environment and the world despite what I went through.
- Another truth is I am worthy to receive and give love.
- Another truth is I *can* love my mother without reservation.

Now that you have gotten to your truths, what do you do with those truths? You start to embrace them by speaking them out loud. If you are like me, I imagine you have swallowed some of your painful truths like bad medicine, leaving a lump in your throat that has lasted most of your life. Remember I just told you that because my secrets were blasted out loud, I developed a coping mechanism to swallow everything and keep it bottled up inside. Developing that coping mechanism only worked temporarily to help me get through some difficult moments. It did not serve me in the best ways in the long run.

I want you to understand that releasing the emotions tied to your hurts will loosen the grip they have on you. It will also physically release the tension in your body in some of the deepest places. One of the coolest things I learned by releasing my truth out loud was I got the benefit of the hurt shrinking in size and releasing the weight it carried in my soul. It was as if my eight-year-old and 14-year-old selves finally had a voice that was heard loud and clear, and we all declared our truths together in unison, healing our past and present while opening the door to our much better future.

As we end this chapter, we are going to work together to build your new truth and value statements to heal your soul. What does this mean? How do you do it? It means you have to learn what you believe about yourself on the inside that you often protect and hide from other people. It is the good that is inside of you that you are afraid to let people see for fear of becoming a victim again. I'll show you what it looks like.

Restoration Blueprint Exercise
Value Statements: "I AM"
Value Statement Examples:

I am beautiful on the inside and out!

I am funny!

I am strong and have nothing to fear!

I am sensitive, and my big heart loves to make people feel special!

I am big and bold!

I am smart and intellectual!

I am love!

Daughters, write your seven value statements starting with "I am…" If you want to have more than seven, by all means, please have as many as you want. I used seven as it represents completion or wholeness in the Bible. Once this is done, I highly recommend putting them on sticky notes on your mirror or any other places where you can see them every day. Each day as you look at them, I want you to say them out loud, not in a whispered voice but in a loud and powerful one. Remember the power you have in your tongue. That is the power I want you to use when saying your "I am" statements. Experts say it takes doing something for 21 days for it to become a habit. But I don't just want this to be a habit; I want these statements to become your core beliefs about yourself. So, don't think of this exercise as habit-building, but as stepping into the truth of who you are. Secondly, let these statements become your daily mantra for your life. Speaking life into ourselves only adds to our self-esteem and boosts our belief in ourselves. The more you say it, the more it gets down into your soul, where you become what you believe. That's how you use the power of your tongue for good.

I can't wait to hear how this exercise affects your soul. Please share your journey with me via my website at www.chequitamccullough.com.

CHAPTER 5

A is for Acceptance of the Past

And he gives grace generously. As the Scriptures say, "God opposes the proud but gives grace to the humble."

—James 4:6, NLT

The difficult truth that your mother was perhaps not the loving, picturesque woman you wanted her to be is a very hard pill to swallow. The scars embedded in your mind, your heart, and in some cases your physical body are constant reminders of this extreme disappointment. In an effort to move forward, you had to learn how to live beyond this painful truth and go on with your life despite the hole in your heart, longing for the ideal mother. On your life journey, you did your best to move into acceptance without the knowledge, emotional aptitude or skill set to do so. When confronted with your experiences in your youth, your underdeveloped mind could not fully comprehend why there was a disconnect or distance with your mother. As you left adolescence behind, you more than likely felt rejected by her, and broken on the inside which led to thoughts and feelings of being less than around your self-image. Those confused feelings you carried inside about the negativity you felt toward your mother also brought forth guilt and shame for thinking them. Looking at your mother through tear-stained eyes sometimes feeling or seeing hate, anger, or resentment where you should have felt love you knew in your heart that your feelings were not right in the eyes of God or your soul.

Conflicting Messages

You muddle through life conflicted and confused, doing the best you can as you ride the river of emotions that is trying to guide you in the right direction. But the waves of hurt, guilt, and shame toss you up and down, round and round, taking you to places you were not meant to be. With these emotions driving your thoughts, you believe that God doesn't like you, because if He did, He would have given you the perfect mother, the mother of the dreams in your hearts, someone suitable to nurture you to become your best self.

The truth is God did not make a mistake when He allowed you to be born through your mother. At birth, you entered an imperfect world filled with imperfect people, just like your mother. The next hard step you must take is looking at how you have been judging your mother from your perspective as a little girl, a judgmental teenager, an insecure young woman, and a confused adult woman. Then you can start to see your mother as God sees you: as an imperfect being worthy of forgiveness and love. You must learn to close the chapters of your past, healing your soul along the way. Every single day, you must allow forgiveness to build up in your heart, mind, and soul until it blossoms into love for your mother. Then you can love her for just being your mother, your giver of life. Hindsight is a powerful tool you can use to look at things in the past and see them as learning points and stepping stones toward the future. You can use these opportunities to build a new framework for what you can do differently going forward with the new skills to help you manage your emotions.

Forgiveness is giving up the hope that the past could be different.
—Dr. Gerald Jampolsky

Your mother is just the vessel who made it possible for you to be here, living and breathing the precious breaths of life that God has given you. You must learn to see the grace that God extends to you every single day and to extend the same measure of grace to your mother. Grace frees you to experience joy, peace, and love while judgment keeps you in bondage to fear, anger, and resentment. God is clear, as John 1:16 (ESV) shows: "And for his fullness we have all received, grace upon grace."

What this shows you is that grace is given again and again. Grace never stops because it is a pivotal steppingstone toward forgiveness. Grace unlocks the door to empathy for you. It helps you put on the stiletto heels of your mother to come to understand her and her own journey prior to becoming your mother. It does not mean you make up excuses as to why you should forgive her; it means you understand some of the places that shaped her into the person she became before you existed.

In most cases, this explains how she showed up in the fashion she did to impact you the way she did as your mother. In my mother's case, there are a lot of secrets in our family. However, what was commonly known and discussed by her and her siblings as we grew up was the extreme abuse, both physical and mental, that they and my grandmother suffered at the hands of my alcoholic grandfather. Sometimes, the family was awakened in the middle of the night by drunken tirades. These could include verbal abuse and even gunfire, sending everyone running for their lives into the darkness, waiting for my grandfather to pass out so they could all come back home and go back to sleep. This plus living in poverty was a deadly combination of fear, lack, humiliation, and constant uncertainty that I know nothing about.

By the time I came into the picture, my experience with my grandfather was one of a loving and gentle man who would bounce me on his knee when I was little and shower me with love and affection until the day he died. I found it hard to believe that the encounters my mother and siblings described could even be associated with my grandfather at all. Unlike the stories about my grandmother's facial damage, the stories about my grandfather all matched in great descriptive detail. How could anyone show emotions or even process emotions in this environment, constantly running in fear for their life?

How did this impact my mother and her siblings? They all became abusers in some way themselves—verbal abusers, physical abusers, or both. The women were primarily verbal abusers, while the men were both. In a weird way, verbal abuse became their love language for one another as siblings, for their spouses, and for their children. To change who you are takes a lot of hard work and many hours of therapy to unpack a lifetime of damage like this. Unfortunately, I know with certainty that my mother and her siblings never sought help to process their experiences and learn how to live differently. They loved in their own way to the best of their ability, which for them was a double-edged sword because they often spoke of wanting their children to have a different experience than they did, which we did to a degree. The saying, "hurt people hurt people" is true for all of us. No one walks on this earth without hurting people along the way. But some of us make a choice to seek help and live life differently.

Grace is Learned, Not Earned

I learned to extend grace to my mother by looking at the circumstances she endured prior to becoming my mother. I tried to picture how my character might have been shaped if I had lived in the environment she lived in every day. I tried to picture hoping to have food on the table to share between eight people and living with a father whose emotions erupted like a volcano, especially when alcohol was the match that lit his fuse. I honestly cannot even wrap my mind around living like that and surviving it, but she did. In talks I have had with her over the years, she told me all she wanted was to give her children a better life than she had. She did that, but it was laced with verbal abuse that left unseen scars on us.

Some of us come away from abuse with destructive behaviors that can be manifested through dependency on drugs, alcohol, or sexual promiscuity. Fortunately, this is not my story, but I know many of you reading this book might have experienced one or all of these along your path. There are many ways to mask feelings of inadequacy outside of drugs, alcohol, and sex. Mine were shopping, eating, and marrying guys who were not capable of loving me due to their issues and my feelings of unworthiness. When you are not mothered, nurtured, or loved by the one who gave you life, it takes a toll on your self-image, which must be reexamined, pulled apart, and reconstructed at some time in your life for you to move to a place of real, authentic self-love.

The Many Facets of Love

I am not saying my mother does or doesn't love me. I believe she does, but that it just does not look and feel the way I would like it to. I have, however, come to accept that what she gives in the ways she gives it is still love. She shows her love for me through what she gives me in material things, like pieces of jewelry she has hand-crafted especially for me. Or when I had to have major surgery and she came to take care of me. For two weeks, she washed and ironed my sheets before making up my bed. I can tell you there is nothing like pressed sheets on your bed, free of wrinkles. I am a "remove from the dryer and place the same sheets back on the bed" kind of girl. In recent years, I have also seen love in her eyes when she looks at me or when I catch her looking at me when she doesn't know I see her. These are all acts and signs of real love. Every now and again, the words "I love you" are even spoken. I am thrown off guard when they are because I was not accustomed to hearing them when I needed to as a child and teenager.

When I started to look for the good in my mother and then tried to find that good inside of me, my acceptance of my past became easier. We all have good and bad sides of us. That is a trait we all share as human beings. Some people show more good than bad and vice versa. We can all make choices as to how we want to project ourselves out into the world. That is where grace comes in. We can choose to show grace, or we can choose to bottle that grace and extend judgment instead.

If we really want to hold onto grievances, we'll never be happy.
It's really a willingness to see the person in the light of love, rather than in the action that happens.

—Dr. Gerald Jampolsky

Grace works in your favor when you accept and give it, and judgment works against you when you dispense it. This is probably the biggest lesson one can learn in life's journey. Moving to acceptance simply because you cannot go back and rewrite your past should be easy to do but is the hardest step to master. Consciously and unconsciously, you want to push the repeat button on your past experiences and hold onto what is not helping you like the security blanket Linus of the Peanuts gang always carried with him. Just like Linus' blanket, holding on to the past will always trip you up. You need to let go of that security blanket and free yourself from its bondage, like a slave chain linking you to your painful past.

Grace Takes Practice

Prayer, meditation, therapy, and putting in the work all help you get to the place where your memories no longer cause you to feel small or like a victim. Grace is letting go of the blame you have heaped upon your mother's shoulders for years, realizing she was doing the best she could, given whatever her circumstances were. When you can use grace to fill the holes in your heart with God's love, grace, and mercy, you can begin the process of removing judgment from your eyes when you look at your mother. Compassion is a great healer because when you show compassion, it can break down barriers, open lines of communication, and build bridges where fractured relationships once lived. Compassion can rebuild a once-crumbled relationship into a dwelling that holds mutual love, respect, and appreciation. Compassion brings miraculous healing to both you and your mother. I believe when you can unravel the past sins you both committed toward one another, you can knit your hearts together in a new pattern that heals even more holes in your hearts.

To prepare you as we move into "Part 2: The Journey to Reconstruct," I want to get you to a space where you can lean into the most critical element: forgiveness. I have prepared an acceptance meditation for you to incorporate as a daily practice as we continue through the remainder of this book and any time you feel you need it. It can also be found on my website. The purpose of this meditation is to get you to a place of peace and calm where you can start to see things objectively about your mother. This is a place where your emotions and thoughts are not running rampant, bringing fear and anxiety into your body and creating blocks and barriers that will keep you from moving forward into forgiveness. This is the most critical step in "Reconstruct to *HEALING*: Letting Go." Remember, you are not alone in this journey. There are many more daughters just like you, going through this journey. We are praying, meditating, and rooting for one another on this journey toward the healing of your heart and soul and the releasing of whatever has been holding you back from being your authentic, powerful, and impactful self. I'll see you in the next chapter with your open minds and hearts ready to let go of these unwanted packages you have been carrying around for decades that have held you back from living your best life. Now, let's meditate.

Acceptance Meditation

Sit comfortably in whatever position works best for you.

Close your eyes.

Start to focus on your breathing.

Take a deep breath in through your nose and gently blow it out through your mouth.

As you continue to breathe in and out slowly, start to feel your body loosen.

Starting at the top of your head, imagine those breaths you just released turning into a soft breeze floating just above your head, just like you feel when a slight breeze is blowing outside.

Now imagine that breeze encircling your head and face.

As you feel the wind on your face, let it carry away the stress that you have been holding in your forehead, behind your eyes, and in your cheeks.

Finally, feel your jaw loosen as the breeze slowly dances around your face.

Now feel the breeze around your neck.

Let it gently caress your neck as it swirls around, releasing the tension as it moves toward your shoulders.

Now feel the breeze encircling your body like a blanket.

As it starts to descend downward, feel the tension releasing from your chest, arms, belly, and up and down your back.

Now feel the breeze sweeping downward onto your thighs, lower legs, and now your feet as you feel it wiggle your toes.

As you feel this, take another deep breath in through your nose and gently blow it out through your mouth.

Repeat these three to five times or however many times you feel you need.

Now sit quietly for a minute or so.

The goal is to sit in complete silence for at least a minute or two to clear your thoughts and those voices in your head.

Repeat your "I am" value statements of acceptance from Chapter 4 and add these five to your list, repeating all of them three times:

I am loved by God.

I am loved by my mother.

I can love myself.

I can love my mother.

I am and have always been worthy to receive and accept love.

Part 2

Journey to Reconstruct

Be kind to one another, tenderhearted, forgiving one another, as God in Christ forgave you.

—Ephesians 4:32

A Prayer of Forgiveness

Dear God,

Oh, great God of forgiveness, we praise Your name.

We know that forgiving others is extremely important to you.

As we move toward forgiveness of ourselves and our mothers, we ask for your sweet grace and mercy yet again.

Forgiveness is one of the hardest places to get to in our hearts and minds.

You are asking us to be tenderhearted, which means opening our hearts and being vulnerable with our mothers, many of whom have wounded the very heart that now has to become tender.

For some of us, this will be easier said than done.

In these times, we know that You will show us how to do it.

We are looking forward to the healing that forgiveness will bring to our souls, to our mothers' souls, and to our relationships with our mothers.

We can already picture in our minds what living with forgiveness in our hearts will look like in this relationship.

Restoration, reconciliation, and love with our mothers have been a lifetime dream since we lost that connection many years ago.

We thank you from the bottom of our healing hearts for helping us realize our dream of reconciliation.

Thank you for Your belief in us and for Your patience with us.

Thank you for always being there for us, even when we felt alone.

Thank you for helping us cross this threshold of complete surrender of unnecessary feelings, guilt, and shame that held us in unforgiveness for so long.

We thank you for the freedom we are about to receive.

We will use our freed state to bless others with the power of forgiveness in Your honor and Your name.

In the matchless name of Jesus Christ. Amen!

CHAPTER 6

L is for Letting Go

Let all bitterness and wrath and anger and clamor and slander be put away from you, along with all malice.

—Ephesians 4:31, ESV

Why does God tell us through Paul to let go of all bitterness, wrath, anger, clamor, slander, and malice as the scripture above shows us? When I went back to look at Ephesians 4, these words leaped off the page: "unity" and "the new life." I discovered that when you let these emotions go there is a sweet reward. You can see the possibilities of what unity with your mother can look like. You get to engage in a relationship with her without the bitterness of the old emotions being front and center. Your heart, mind, and ears are no longer clouded with judgment keeping you from seeing the possibility of a relationship with your mother. These shady emotions once had you trapped in a cage you built for protection, leaving you too frightened to take a step out and live powerfully. In the process of letting go, you move into the light of who you truly are. This frees you from the past and brings you into a place of peace.

As I read Ephesians 4, I saw this in verses 1-3: ". . . walk in a manner worthy of the calling to which you have been called, with all humility and gentleness, with patience, bearing with one another in love, eager to maintain the unity of the Spirit in the bond of peace." For me, this explained why my soul was never at peace and why I could never fix my relationship with my mother all the other times I tried.

Unlocking Forgiveness with New Tools

You cannot get to unity, love, and peace with bitterness, wrath, anger, clamor, slander, and malice as your tools of choice. Doing this is like bringing gasoline and a match to put out a major fire. It simply will not work. For you to heal and rebuild your relationship with your mother, you must obtain the proper tools of humility, gentleness, love, and the spirit of peace. One of the other things you must do is step out of your nature, which is the behaviors you have formulated over time, and rebuild a new life for yourself so that your life reflects what Ephesians 4 tells you about in verses 17-32.

Let's look at the tools we get to build our new life. When we gave our life to Christ, we were supposed to give up our old ways that were not serving us well like our futile minds and the ignorance of our hardened and calloused hearts because we were taught the truth in Jesus to "put off our old self which belongs to our former manner of life and be renewed in the spirit of our minds, and put on our new self, created in the likeness of God." Did we do that? No. We committed to Jesus but kept our old self because it was much easier to hold on to the tools that supported our blame game toward our mothers.

Verse 25 contains the long list of things He told us we were not to do, yet we continued doing them and getting terrible results in our lives, often wondering why or how we got to the places we were not supposed to be. Verse 31 once again gives us clear direction with verse 32 reminding us of the benefits that happen when we let go of the old and embrace the new. "Let all bitterness and wrath and anger and clamor and slander be put away from you, along with all malice. Be kind to one another, tenderhearted, forgiving one another, as God in Christ forgave you."

When I got to this place, I really had to examine whether I had forgiven my mother. Why was I still doing things that blocked my ability to fully forgive her for what I had experienced in her care? I remember I tried to confront my mother about my feelings and experiences before I had the tools to do it properly. The operative word here was "confront." Whenever we attempt to confront something, it typically means we have our own agenda and that it is the only one that matters to us.

The Cost of Unforgiveness

My purpose and intention for this first attempt was to make my mother hear how she had hurt me. I did not care about what she had to say or how she felt; this was about how she messed me up, and I wanted to let her know just how terrible she had been as a mother, and that I was her walking damaged package. Bitterness, wrath, anger, clamor, and malice all wove tightly together, being sprayed by my tongue like bullets. In the Oxford Pocket dictionary, "clamor" is defined as "a loud and confused noise, especially that of people shouting vehemently." This is exactly what our conversation looked like. Instead of words of repentance, humility, gentleness, and love being spoken, she got bitterness . . . take that! Wrath . . . take that! Clamor, clamor, clamor . . . take that! Slander . . . take that! Malice . . . take that! I came at her with tongue blazing, further inflaming the situation.

I had a good teacher to demonstrate how to use my words in a hurtful way. I learned this from her. What I had forgotten was my mother's history of verbal abuse at the hands of her father. She was trained, ready, and well-equipped to fire back more ferociously than I ever could. When the dust settled from this shouting match over the phone, I scurried away, more tattered than ever before, I retreated by hanging up on her, and in the click of the phone call, I tried to regain my power, as futile as it was. I wasn't the victor in this fight; I was once again a victim. The truth is in this instance, we were both victims.

This failed attempt was a disaster and subsequently created a three-year gap, during which my mother and I did not speak a word to each other. There was no hello, no goodbye, no small talk—nothing. We literally did not acknowledge each other's existence. This put a major strain on our family, including my son, the only grandchild in the family.

The Journey Through Unforgiveness

This incident was born out of something that happened many years before. The click of the phone that I had originally wanted to heal did more damage than good. It was the cherry on top of our tumultuous relationship that began when I was 14. Remember I told you about my mother breaking all the privacy rules when I started my period. Well, that escalated into weeks and months of us arguing back and forth about anything and everything under the sun. I could not get her to see my point about the invasion of privacy. Her stance was that, while I was living in her house, I was not entitled to privacy; everything was fair game. I tried to have a locked diary once, but she broke the lock and read my private thoughts, then ridiculed me about them.

Out of frustration, I wrote a letter to one of my closest friends about constantly fighting with my mother. In this letter, I said, *"My mother is acting like a BITCH and getting on my last nerve!"* At 14, I did not think this letter or its contents would ever get back to my mother. God's Word shows up in moments when you least expect it. Here was Ephesians 4:31 strewn all through the letter about my mother, stamped with one of the most inflammatory words to women, to a mother from her daughter: "BITCH." At school the next day, I gave the letter to my friend. By the end of the day, my mother not only knew the contents of this letter but had it in her possession. What?! How in the h-e-double toothpicks did that happen?!

My friend's mother had found the letter among her daughter's possessions, called my mother, and read it to her. Then my mother drove to her house and took possession of it. I guess my friend did not have any privacy rights either. From this point forward for decades, we were a pair of combustible elements, waiting to explode at any given moment. This period left a trail of scars and bruises on our souls that would take years to heal and mend. I believe to this day my mother still has this letter because over the years it has come up. I really wish she would let it go by throwing it away but that is her road, not mine. I clearly remember apologizing to my mother about using the word "bitch" as she waved the letter in my face. This letter was obviously a huge mistake, and it never should have been written.

My mother clung to that letter and practically wore it like a brooch on her clothes when she interacted with me, constantly reminding me how I had hurt her by hurting me with her words. It never occurred to me how deeply that word hurt my mother until my son hurled it at me when he was about the same age I was when I used it. In that moment,

I felt the proverbial slap to the face and sucker punch to the gut that shook everything inside of me and the extreme disempowerment of that inflammatory word. In that moment, I finally stood in the same stiletto heels my mother had, crying in my soul that my child could use such a horrible word and aim it at me. The difference between me and my mother was that, while she held it over my head, I used it to understand what I had done to make my son feel that way about me. I used it to heal my relationship with my son, not to destroy it. I chose to fight for love, not build up negative feelings. I chose to use Ephesians 4:32 as my guidepost to be tender-hearted and forgive one another, as God in Christ forgave me.

Perhaps some of you reading this chapter cannot imagine not speaking to your mother, especially for years. Others of you reading this book may have had a longer period of silence than I did and may still be in silence in your relationship. All I can speak about is what my experience was during this time. In my righteous indignation, I wore bitterness, wrath, anger, clamor, slander, and malice like the badges I received on my sash when I was a Girl Scout, front and center, every single day. I refused to see how I had hurt my mother all those years ago. I instead chose to constantly add fuel to that fire again and again, then later in life blame her for all kinds of poor choices I made.

Writing that letter was a poor choice that had substantial repercussions attached to it. Giving it to my friend was a poor choice. What I discovered was that I had to let go of the narrative I had built around how my mother did or didn't love me. Where would my relationship with my mother be if I had not written that letter? I will never know. Would our relationship have been as tumultuous as it was? I don't know. Do I wish she had handled it like I did with my son? Of course, but that is not our story.

To Cancel or Not to Cancel

Our story has taken many years to get to where it is today, where there is mutual respect, love, and understanding. Is it perfect? No, it is not. Is it better than it was? Yes, absolutely. Has my mother changed? Some, but mostly she is the same—still very fiery with her words and her explosions of anger. The difference is that I have changed. I chose to let go of the bitterness, wrath, anger, clamor, slander, and malice and accept God's principle of forgiveness, which leads to love, reconciliation, and restoration, uniting all areas of my life. My journey to get to the place where I could let go of my experiences from the past with my mother was through prayer, meditation, journaling, therapy, and actual real-time engagement with my mother with a new perspective set on a foundation of love and admiration for her as my mother, the giver of my life.

Today, we live in a culture that tells us to permanently remove anyone from our universe who is not meeting our expectations or who has hurt us. I am not saying this is right or wrong. I am simply offering a different perspective—the God perspective. God's perspective is always around restoration and unity, especially within the family dynamic. If we are following Jesus as our life model, how can we cancel people out of our lives? Did Jesus permanently cancel anyone? No. Time and time again, He forgave and loved the most difficult people. He loved those who had never experienced love themselves and, in turn, had hurt others. If you can look at your relationship with your mother through God's lens, then I believe you will start to see and believe that there is the possibility of healing and restoration in your relationship too. Think about it this way: what might the costs be if you do not try to restore this very important relationship? What will it cost you? What will it cost your child and future generations?

Is canceling your mother permanently worth the price for your future and the future of your family?

The Gift of Forgiveness

As I said above, I tried to cancel my relationship with my mother, long before it became popular to do so. However, something in my soul would not allow it. I was completely restless and filled with turmoil during the three years during which I had no connection with my mother. I am so glad that I didn't leave things there. Once I began to show and express forgiveness toward myself and my mother, my life completely changed. Once I let it all go, my life shifted. I felt peace, joy, love, and gratitude within like I had never felt before. I believe it propelled me onto the journey I am on today. I have never looked back in regret at what might have been because I am living in the present, grateful every day for what I do have in my life.

Once I made this shift, my relationships with my family and friends became richer. My career blossomed, my creativity soared, my confidence grew, and my purpose became crystal clear. I believe all these areas of my life were overshadowed and diminished greatly by my unforgiving heart. Once I moved into real forgiveness, my life exploded in abundant gifts in all areas. In fact, I'll share a story that was so miraculous, I still have a hard time wrapping my head around it.

I was born with a heart murmur that was not discovered until I was 16. At the age of 25, I started having chest palpitations and irregular heartbeats. After visiting with my doctor for an annual checkup, it was discovered, following a battery of tests, that I had a condition called mitral valve prolapse, which is a heart valve disease. I was put on medication that I would have to take for the rest of my life. This condition can be developed at any age, so I am not sure when or how it developed. Nonetheless, I had to learn to live with it, and I did.

Fast-forward to my mid-forties. I went to my annual physical appointment as I do every year. In speaking with my doctor, I reminded her that I needed to have the medication refilled for this condition. She then asked a weird question: "Why are you taking this medication?" The reason she asked this was that she was not the physician who had found the condition. It had been diagnosed 20 years prior. But since being in her care, we had never discussed it. She had me go through a series of tests again to validate the previous findings. When the test results came back, she called me in for an office visit and revealed that there were no signs of mitral valve prolapse at all and said I should immediately stop taking any of the medication for it. It was a miracle, to say the least. A medically documented miracle. I like to think that God healed my heart because of the courageous move I made to heal my relationship with my mother. I cannot prove it, but I know that all things are possible when God is involved. I believe my healing is in direct correlation to my forgiveness muscle being exercised. My heart is now a place where love flows. When I held onto unforgiveness, love could not flow through that broken vessel.

I believe that forgiveness brings healing to many parts of our lives mentally, physically, and spiritually. Forgiveness has amazing power, and there is a multitude of gifts we get to experience as a result of exercising forgiveness, both for ourselves and toward others. My story is amazing, and I am grateful that my heart was literally restored to health. The question is: what could be restored in your life because you learned to forgive and walk in love? Take inspiration and courage from my experience to find out what could happen for you and your mother.

Let's examine how the words of Ephesians 4:31 might show up in your thoughts, stories, and emotions, based on your past experiences with your mother. This is an important step for you because before you can let go, you need to first have an honest conversation with yourself to see where you are. Once you get this picture, you can do some work to change your outlook and your narrative, to empower yourself to move toward changing who you want to be and how you want to show up in the world. You can then begin rebuilding that relationship on your terms without your mother.

It's time to add to your Restoration Blueprint. Get yourself ready to let go of your thoughts, stories, and emotions and build new thoughts, stories, and emotions where your mother is concerned. Go to a clean page in your journal or companion guide, and at the top of the page write the words, "It's Time to Let it ALL Go!" Let those words sink in for a bit.

Let's break this apart and put it back together in your blueprint! Let's Reveal and Reconstruct!

Let all bitterness and wrath and anger and clamor and slander be put away from you, along with all malice.

—Ephesians 4:31, ESV

Now, let's go to our Restoration Blueprint and get into the next exercise to help us *Reconstruct* our thoughts, stories, emotions, and resentment, based on the new experiences you want to have with your mother. In other words, let's make your intentional plan toward real forgiveness of yourself and your mother. For this exercise, you are only going to focus on yourself and your mother. Get your journals or companion guides and go to a clean page. At the top of that page, write the words, "Reconstruct My Mindset." Write on one side of the page, "love, joy, peace, patience, kindness, goodness, faithfulness, gentleness, self-control." Following the description below, build statements next to each word for yourself and then for your mother.

Restoration Blueprint
Reveal and Let Go Exercise—Example

Describe how these emotions have impacted your
relationship with yourself.
(Insecurity, Self-doubt, Self-loathing, Fear, etc.)

Bitterness: Bitterness showed up as not feeling good enough in
every situation.

Wrath: Wrath showed up as the need to make others around me feel
miserable.

Anger: Anger showed up as intentionally hurting people's feelings.

Clamor: Clamor showed up as always talking over people so I could
be heard.

Slander: Slander showed up in me being highly critical and judgmental
of others.

Malice: Malice was my intentional act to hurt others' feelings under
the banner of speaking my truth.

Letting Go Exercise #1

Describe how these have impacted your relationship with yourself.
(Insecurity, Self-doubt, Self-loathing, Fear, etc.)

Bitterness: _____

_____

Wrath: _____

_____

Anger: _____

_____

Clamor: _____

_____

Slander: _____

_____

Malice: _____

_____

Break emotions down by people here as well as others not listed that you would like to address.
(Mother/Father/Siblings, Spouse/Significant Other/Children)

Bitterness: _____

_____

Wrath: _____

_____

Anger: _____

_____

Clamor: _____

_____

Slander: _____

_____

Malice: _____

_____

Describe how these have impacted your relationships in your work/career and community.

(Co-workers/Workplace/Church/Friendships, etc.)

Bitterness: _____

_____

Wrath: _____

_____

Anger: _____

_____

Clamor: _____

_____

Slander: _____

_____

Malice: _____

_____

Restoration Blueprint
Reconstruct My Mindset (Self)—Example

Following the example below, describe how you want to see yourself showing up in the world every day, walking in the Fruit of the Spirit (Gal. 5:22-23).

Love: When I look in the mirror each day, I want to love what I see and the person I have become.

Joy: When I wake up in the morning, I want to feel joy in my soul.

Peace: As I go throughout the day, I want to feel peace in my soul.

Patience: I want to feel patience with myself by not striving for perfection.

Kindness: I want to feel the kindness inside of me being extended to others through me.

Goodness: I want to extend goodness to constantly have a positive impact on other people.

Faithfulness: I want to trust God in everything, especially the things I cannot control.

Gentleness: I want the gentleness in my soul to be nurturing and soothing to others.

Self-Control: I want to practice self-control so I can maintain my joy, peace, kindness, goodness, and love.

Reconstruct My Mindset (Mother)—Example

Using the example below, describe how you want to see your relationship with your mothers through the Fruit of the Spirit (Gal 5.22).

Love: When I engage with my mother, I want to lean in to hear the words that express her love for me and accept her love in the way it is delivered.

Joy: When I engage with my mother, I want to listen to her words and seek the joy in them that she expresses about me.

Peace: When I engage with my mother, I will cherish the engagements where we laugh and cry together.

Patience: When I engage with my mother, I remember that neither she nor I is a perfect being, and that we will still make mistakes from time to time.

Kindness: When I feel my mother extend acts of kindness toward me, I will accept them for what they are and not look for hidden motives.

Goodness: I will intentionally look for the goodness in my mother because some of her goodness is also in me.

Faithfulness: I will continually pray for the wellbeing of my mother and pray she too experiences healing in her soul.

Gentleness: I will reflect often on the moments of gentleness I have experienced with my mother and treat them as the cherished gifts they are.

Self-Control: I will help my mother learn my boundaries, which will help us to be successful in our engagements and maintain balance in our relationship.

Paul says in Romans, "And we know that for those who love God all things will work together for good, for those who are called according to his purpose." (Romans 8:28) When you submit all your hurts, your broken heart, and your painful memories to this promise, God shows you that these hurts can and will be used for good. This book is a representation of this for me. My relationship with my mother is a testimony to this promise as well. Use this promise as leverage as you move into the next chapter to "Ignite Self-Love" to grow and become your authentic selves. I cannot wait to hear how these exercises went for you. Reach out to me via my website at www.chequitamccullough.com.

CHAPTER 7

I is for Ignite Self-Love

Is not my word like fire, declares the LORD, and like a hammer that breaks the rock in pieces?

—Jeremiah 23:29, ESV

The barriers you have built around your heart toward your mother have to be broken to allow your mother to fully receive your love, and for you to pour it out fully toward your mother. You have spent the past few chapters building your awareness of how you feel, how you show up, and how you perceive your mother. You have completed a few exercises to gain awareness and start to look at your relationship with your mother through the eyes of forgiveness—of yourself and your mother. This is a critical choice and a turning-point moment. You can choose to let go of your judgmental thoughts, your critical eyes, your resentment-filled heart, and your combustible actions, or you can continue to wrap yourself in these old places of familiarity that continue to block you from becoming who you really want to be.

The goal here is to walk in forgiveness, both for yourself and toward your mother. Forgiveness is a huge life marker for many. A lack of forgiveness can keep people stuck for their entire lives, rehashing and holding onto hurt, and lost forever. It destroys your mental, emotional, and physical state, keeping you stunted in your growth and development as a human being. In the Bible, depending on which version you are reading, there are between 95 and 200 references to forgiveness. Jesus even asked God to forgive the people who nailed Him to the cross before His last breath was taken.

The Power of Forgiveness

As Christians, if we do not understand the significance or importance of forgiveness in our lives, then why are we calling ourselves Christians? We can make up all the excuses we want like, "I ain't Jesus," and the host of other things we have been saying to ourselves, but the fact is that, as Christ-followers, we are called to live differently than the rest of the world. Forgiveness is a major principle in the Christian life. Let's stop being convenient Christians who loosely forgive people when it fits our agenda and start living life through the full forgiveness of others.

Forgiveness restores our mental peace, rebuilds our emotional state, and even restores our physical bodies from the wear and tear that the stress of unforgiveness can cause. This makes it an important part of our self-care and self-love processes. Scientists and medical professionals have been telling us for decades how holding onto unforgiveness breaks down the molecular structure within our bodies causing all types of illnesses and diseases like depression, anxiety, autoimmune disorders, cardiovascular disease, chronic pain, and many others. The article "Forgiveness: Your Health Depends on It" from *Johns Hopkins Medicine* shows the benefits of forgiveness. "Studies have found that the act of forgiveness can reap huge rewards for your health, lowering the risk of heart attack; improving cholesterol levels and sleep; and reducing pain, blood pressure, and levels of anxiety, depression, and stress" (John Hopkins Medicine).

There are many books and resources available to enlighten you on the benefits of forgiveness, some of which I have listed for you in the back of this book. As a coach, I have observed ways in which unforgiveness shows up in our thoughts, emotions, and actions as we try to walk on our life journey. In my personal experience, unforgiveness has had mental effects as well as physical ones, such as migraines and weight gain from eating my way through painful mental emotions of not being good enough, again trying to alter my physical appearance to become ugly because I did not feel accepted by my mother. I was attempting to run away from the problem of living in unforgiveness rather than learning how to process those mental and physical effects and learn to deal with them and extend forgiveness.

For years before I started to learn about the power of forgiveness and the toll unforgiveness takes on our mental, emotional, and physical states, I would frequently get severe migraines that required high doses of medication to help them subside. My doctors could never find a reason or trigger for them, and while I cannot make a direct correlation, they gradually disappeared as I worked through therapy, prayer, and meditation. Not only did I no longer experience migraines, but I found that real joy, peace, and happiness entered my life the minute I started to really work on forgiveness in my life. I now believe that the unrest I felt toward my mother was the root of tension that flowed through my body and landed in my head in the form of migraines.

In therapy, I learned to feel my feelings. I also learned how and where my emotions were showing up in my physical body.

For example, fear shows up in my chest like tremendous pressure, as though someone is stepping on my lungs and pushing the air out of them. I learned to process my feelings in healthy ways, not by stuffing them down but by facing them, sitting with them, and riding the wave of emotional processing until I could constructively resolve their cause. You too can get invaluable tools like the ones my therapist gave me, such as "Feeling My Feelings" and "Anxiety Defense Triangle," both of which are in the resource section of this book. These tools were life-changing for me and can help you gain clarity and get you to a healthier state of being.

Emotional Intelligence

Learning to use these tools to process my feelings in healthy ways has not only made my relationship with my mother better but has also translated into better relationships overall. These tools blew the door open for me to start forgiving myself and my mother. The biggest benefit of forgiveness for me is that it opens me up to express love more fully. I often wonder what my life would have looked like if I'd had these tools in my 20s and 30s. God always gives us the information we need. The problem is often that we are not open or ready to receive it when it is given. However, we will get there sooner or later. When I finally was able to receive the information God was giving me, it resonated with several issues I was working through that had been holding me back. Once I changed my mindset, the door opened to the possibility of doing things differently.

The key is getting to a space of openness that will allow you to make mental shifts in the direction of forgiveness. I want you to learn what feelings you have trapped under the unforgiveness you feel toward yourself, which may be strongly tied to your mother. I want women to learn to process their emotions in healthy ways and learn tools to effectively manage their emotional and mental state so they can move beyond the mismanagement of emotions. This will allow them to rise, stand up, and live out a better version of themselves through authenticity.

It is so worth all the pain and tears of processing the feelings to get to a place of acceptance, leaving those old emotions in the past where they belong. Let's be truthful here: you will never forget your painful experiences, but you do not have to continue to lug the emotions attached to those experiences around you. After all, what benefit have you been getting from holding on to painful emotions? Whatever perceived benefits you have been holding onto are not really benefits at all, because they have not been serving you well. Women will come to realize they don't have to hold on to hurt and emotions that are not serving them powerfully. They can move forward into forgiveness with confidence, living healthy, authentic lives, and experiencing the joy, peace, and happiness they have longed for every day.

As you learn how to grow in love, you allow the person who has been trampled and hindered inside for years to show up in the world. Just as a cocooned caterpillar emerges as a beautiful butterfly, you too can appear after having spent time manifesting into a beautiful creation for the world to see. This is where you must allow God to do His wonderful and marvelous work. When He can change you, it typically starts on the inside and then moves outward. Like a glass blower, breathing air on the inside, as the outer shape gets spun in the fire taking on a new form and shape. God's reshaping fire does not scorch you; it turns you into a brilliant gem that shines by allowing

His light in you to illuminate your healed soul. It repairs your broken heart with artistry using His divine hammer, breaking your hardened heart into pieces only to restore it with His love and care. He then melts the broken pieces back together and blows them into a fully healed and whole heart that can now forgive and love yourself and your mother.

A healed mind also supports your emotional intelligence by replacing your judgmental thoughts with thoughts of respect. Removing judgment that previously clouded your vision allows you to see with the eyes of love and discover clear truths. God rebuilds your resentful heart as a heart of empathy and compassion. I would never have gotten to experience these things if I had not submitted and leaned into what God was trying to teach me about my judgmental, critical, resentful, and combustible actions. Every time I tried to take a step in the right direction without Him, I only made matters worse because I would not listen and was not equipped to successfully transform myself. This was because my focus was on my mother and getting her to change, not on what or how I needed to change.

Our Areas of Responsibility

When I try to change things that are beyond my control, my friend who is a judge likes to say, "That is not in your jurisdiction." Changing my mother is out of my jurisdiction. If she needs to change, that is something God will tend to, not me. Though it seems we are always trying to do God's work, we are well out of our jurisdiction when we do so. The truth is that neither you nor I have the power to make anyone change. The only person we can change is ourselves. I had to come to the place of accepting that I had no control over anyone's actions but my own. Control freak that I am, this was a hard pill to swallow. But my friend is right—changing someone is not in my jurisdiction. It is in God's.

My responsibility is to change myself and myself alone. We must stop thinking we can change others and focus solely on where our responsibility actually lies. When we focus on ourselves, God does the miraculous and starts to show us what our lives can look like as we gradually take steps in the right direction. Along the way, God is healing us, removing barriers we have placed in our own way as boundaries of protection, like the walls of Jericho. God gives us opportunities crafted to test out our new selves along the way, building our confidence as we go and showing us that we have the strength and intellect to approach this new path without fearing the worst. This is because all things are possible with God. Even if for some reason we find that we cannot restore our relationships with our mothers, that is not a reflection on us. It just means God is still working on opening our mothers' hearts and minds to allow them to see who their daughters are becoming.

Changing Before Your Very Eyes

As one who has walked and is continuing to walk this path, I can tell you that when you start to see the image of your mother changing in front of your very eyes, there is nothing like it. She may have always been there, but perhaps you were not ready or could not see it because of the old lens through which you were looking at her. When you start to look at her through the eyes of forgiveness, the truth comes through. You begin to discover things you never knew about her. You begin to have different experiences with her. When you humble yourself to not judge her because of her human frailty, she becomes a great mystery that you want to discover. You move to a place of surrender and curiosity about her. You start to look for the good pieces of her that are in you. You start to awaken to a new sense of yourself. Stripping away the old allows the new to be revealed. It's like a piece of furniture that still has good bones but needs to be restored for a new purpose. When we are restored, we find new purpose.

Now let's dig into what forgiveness really is versus what we may have learned or been told it is. When we gain our understanding from the biblical perspective, we are set up for true success to happen. For this we can look at a lesson James, the brother of Jesus, teaches us in James 5:16 (ESV). He says, "Therefore, confess your sins to one another and pray for one another, that you may be healed. The prayer of a righteous person has great power as it is working." First, we see the word, "confess" which means to admit with reluctance that there is a problem. Second, pray not only for yourself but for others to gain healing in this area. Lastly, through prayer, there is great power that leads to healing and the release of forgiveness. This means that as you seek to forgive others and speak about it, healing can begin through your words.

Here is another scripture on forgiveness to help solidify your perspective. Luke 6:37 says, "Judge not, and you will not be judged; condemn not, and you will not be condemned; forgive, and you will be forgiven . . ." This scripture contains the three areas that hold us back from being fully open to love, especially loving ourselves fully. The judgment, condemnation, and unforgiveness we point in the direction of our mothers sit squarely on our shoulders and affect how we view ourselves. When we can release others from unforgiveness, the real benefit is that we can finally move to release ourselves.

Let's go to your Restoration Blueprint. Pull out your journal or companion guide. Now it is time to start unpacking this for you. Here are some questions that I want you to answer as you dig into why you are holding onto unforgiveness where your mother is concerned. Go to a quiet place as you ponder these next questions. Capture everything that comes up for you and write it down. It might not mean anything in this moment, but it may give you clues to help you look deeper.

In Chapter 3, "Hard Steps," I had you answer a few questions. The answer you wrote to question #2, "Which emotions do you find it hardest to accept when you think about your relationship with your mother?" This is a great place to look for unforgiveness. Often, things that are hard to accept are the places that are held onto tightly. Use the answers that you wrote down to this question as your starting place. As you begin to work on reframing these emotions through the lens of forgiveness and love, I want you to think about and answer the next questions.

How are you now empowered to let go of those thoughts and emotions that you held onto in your relationship with your mother?
What is different for you now?
What do you believe now that you did not believe before?
Write out what is true for you today.
What is now allowing you to open the door to complete forgiveness in these areas?

Pull in your truth and value statements here as well. You are building up your pillars of truth to gain real forgiveness. All of the tools thus far are necessary to get to the end result of forgiveness, which is where you want to be. Remember the question in Chapter 3, "What will it take for you to trust and let go of your past experiences?"

Think about this for just a moment...just on the other side of letting go is forgiveness. You have come this far; don't stop at the threshold and look through the door. Do this work and kick that door open for yourself. You have been empowered to do so.

The goal of these exercises in this chapter is to change your perspective on the unforgiveness you are harboring by becoming open and truthful in the process to see your situation from a different perspective and move to total forgiveness. If we are using God as our frame of reference for forgiveness, I am sure you will be led to the place of forgiveness you need. I am also going to share an additional resource tool given to me by my therapist. It may help you go even deeper to get some clarity and needed answers and uproot unforgiveness. I have placed it in the resource section of the book. It is called the "Four Phases of Forgiveness" from Therapist Aid, LLC (2017).

Now that you have completed the exercises, let's do a little reflection. With all the work you did from the exercises above and using the forgiveness worksheets if needed, I want you to reflect and write to capture what happened as you completed this exercise for this chapter.

What did you discover about forgiveness?
What was most challenging about the process?

How did the process empower you to change your emotions and beliefs regarding forgiveness?

How did the process prepare you to reengage your emotions toward your mother?

I will be praying for your soul restoration. I'll see you in the next chapter, where we will start to enlist your mother in this healing and reconciliation process.

I am excited to hear how these exercises went for you. Reach out to me with your thoughts and comments via my website at www.chequitamccullough.com.

Forgive others, not because they deserve forgiveness, but because you deserve peace.

—Jonathan Lockwood Muir

CHAPTER 8

N is for Navigate Your Healing Relationship

Finally, brothers and sisters, whatever is true, whatever is noble, whatever is right, whatever is pure, whatever is lovely, whatever is admirable—if anything is excellent or praiseworthy—think about such things. Whatever you have learned or received or heard from me, or seen in me—put it into practice. And the God of peace will be with you.

—Philippians 4:8-9, NIV

This scripture represents a few of God's key principles for our lives. Whatever is true, noble, pure, lovely, and admirable, these are attributes of God, Jesus, and the Holy Spirit. These are also attributes that have been given to us by the Holy Spirit. The challenge for us as humans is accepting that we have the capability to embody these attributes and live a life that represents them in the public eye. Society has taught us that showing these types of attributes makes us weak and pushovers when the complete opposite is true. These attributes make us more powerful and helpful to our fellow human beings. They also act as our internal compass to allow us to have compassion for others.

They help us bridge the gap to get reconciliation, restoration, and peace on Earth, or at least in our own environments. These are the attributes that can take a lifetime of practice to get right. Luke 17:3-4 (NIV) is clear: "So watch yourselves. If your brother or sister sins against you, rebuke them; and if they repent, forgive them. Even if they sin against you seven times in a day and seven times come back to you saying, 'I repent,' you must forgive them." Forgiveness must be a consistent practice in our daily lives.

As verse 9 of Philippians 4 shows us, our objective is to continually practice these attributes that will lead us to a place of peace within our being. Our practice will lead us to a time when our practiced actions become praiseworthy events and show the excellence of God. We are all searching for peace on the inside as well as the outside. When we practice and fail, we are forgiven and given another opportunity to practice again. When we practice and succeed, we get to experience another attribute of God: His perfect peace.

Practicing for Confidence

Implementing these principles will take a lot of daily practice. When you are engaging with other people throughout your daily life, you will have opportunities that will challenge your thoughts, feelings, and actions based on where you are in the moment. If someone is talking to you disrespectfully, are you going to lash back or try to understand their motives and extend grace and compassion? These life moments allow you to practice choosing to either represent the love of Jesus or allow your ego to override. In this journey, you will stumble and fall, but you must get back on the right side and keep practicing.

We have learned from God what we are called to do. We have received from God many blessings simply because He loves each of us. These blessings were not earned by our actions but were freely given to us because of who we are. We are His. We have heard the Holy Spirit's words in the thoughts in our heads and heartstrings pulling us on the side of doing right, trying to shield us from doing wrong. We have seen what this practice looks like when it was demonstrated by Jesus when He stood up for the woman being stoned for her wrongs. When was the last time we stepped in to help someone who was in need, instead of filming the wrong on our phone to post? Another example is when Jesus intervened between siblings Martha and Mary. He helped Martha see that because of her focus, she was creating anxiety and trouble where there should have been peace, while Mary sat at Jesus' feet in the place of peace. Often, we create the issues that keep us from the places of happiness, peace, and joy because of the things we are doing that we do not realize.

When you learn to live in a state of self-awareness regarding your thoughts, emotions, and actions and understand how they drive you, then you can learn to self-govern your actions and get to the outcome you are seeking, which is a place of happiness, peace, and joy. You cannot get there when you are worked up and emotional. You cannot get to a better relationship with your mother by continually playing the reel of old hurts over and over. This will never get you to a place of peace within yourself or with your mother.

Navigating The Healing Journey

In order to heal, you must embark on the healing journey that takes you to a place of peace within yourself. When you are at peace with yourself and with your mother, this is the place where new hope lives, where you can begin healing this critical relationship. To prepare you to enter peace with your mother, I have written an example of a love letter to all mothers from the collective voices of daughters reading this book. After you read this one, you will complete an exercise where you write your own love letter in your own words. You will be writing this letter twice. The intention of this exercise is for you to write down all the emotions and feelings you have about your relationship. But first, you will sit with this letter and process through it. This letter represents in written form all of the words you have always wanted to say but never got the opportunity to express.

You may get angry, you may cry, and you may even feel despair. All of this is expected because you are clearing out the place where these wounds have lain hidden deep inside of you, tearing you apart from the inside out. Then you will rewrite your love letter to your mother as an expression of your love for her despite your past relationship.

You are writing this letter because, for some of you, speaking these words directly to your mother would be a difficult task without having processed through the scenario first. You may be triggered by the emotional recall of how you have felt during your relationship with your mother. You may struggle to find words to match the intention of your heart to get into a better relationship with your mother. You may feel like you cannot formulate the words to honestly convey what you might want to say. Up to this point, you may have never expressed your true feelings to anyone about your relationship, let alone directly to your mother. Instead, you have held most of the words inside of you. It is time to let these words and experiences go so they will no longer have the power they once had over you. It is time for you to shed the pain and memories of these hurts and step out, allowing your light to shine for the world to see. You are bold, courageous, and beautiful, and everyone needs to experience the real you, full of life and love.

For some of you, even after you write your heartfelt love letter, you may still feel you can't give it to your mother or have a conversation about it out of fear of how she might react. I want you to know that feeling like this is perfectly okay. Trust me on this one. Writing this letter was life-changing for me and then for my relationship with my mother. I want this for you too. You should know that after writing my own letter, I was completely fearful and unsure of what would happen if I gave her the letter. Remember she still has the original letter that was the epicenter of the breakdown of our relationship.

I chose not to give her the letter for one simple reason: I did not want her to place this letter with the other one in her personal treasure chest of memories. I envisioned her adding this letter right on top of the other one, which is exactly what I did not want to happen. I wanted this new letter to stand on its own merit as a representation of what I thought about her now. So instead, I decided to live out my love letter toward my mother one piece at a time until we got to a place where we would interact with love and respect toward one another. My mother got to experience my letter in real time. I did this because I knew my mother was not the kind of person who responded to affirming words. Based on her past life experience, this is very uncomfortable for her. I believed, however, that she could respond in kind to different and more loving behaviors exhibited by me toward her, which is exactly what happened over time. Where's my letter? It resides in my secret treasure chest. I use it on those days when I need a reminder of the triumph over a very difficult past with my mother and as my secret weapon to maintain my internal peace.

Here is my example of the open expression of a love letter to all mothers on behalf of all daughters. In this letter, I am preparing our mothers' hearts as well as ours to receive the love and openness we are trying to re-establish with them. Sometimes, words from a stranger can be powerful and open up hearts to receive what may not be received from someone close to us. Let this letter be a key to unlocking our hearts and minds to begin an ever-evolving and growing relationship with our mothers. Feel free to use this letter to start a conversation with your mother, as it may give her the context of why you are doing what you are doing. I don't want it to be used in place of your letter but in support of it.

There may be some of you reading this book whose mothers are no longer here. There still can be healing for you, too, through this exercise. I invite you to continue the exercise; however, you will be doing your presentation of this letter differently. This exercise for you will be about expressing gratitude for you coming into the world through her, releasing forgiveness toward your mother, and healing current and future generations in your family.

Here are a few suggestions for you to present your letter:

1. Take flowers to her gravesite, pray or meditate, and read it to her.
2. Go into your prayer closet, pray or meditate, and read it aloud.
3. Go to a favorite place of hers, pray or meditate, and read it aloud.
4. Go to your favorite place, pray or meditate, and read it aloud.

5. Do a burn ritual in which you read it aloud then burn it as a symbol of letting go and stepping into forgiveness for both of you.

The point here is to pick a place that is special, peaceful, or calming for you as you take this important healing step. After completing this exercise in this chapter, you will be focused for the rest of the book on healing yourself, your family, and future generations through this journey.

A Love Letter of Reconciliation for Our Mothers

Dear Mothers,

Thank you for bringing us into this world. We are grateful for what you did to bring us here. We acknowledge that at some point in our life journey, we separated in spirit and in our physical connection as mother and daughter. Our heart's desire is to reconnect with you and rebuild our relationship on a strong foundation of mutual respect, trust, and love. As we move forward to work with you to rebuild our relationships, there is one thing that we ask of you.

Please understand that, as fully grown adults, we don't need a parent; we need a mother. At this stage in our lives, we want you to be an advisor, an advocate, and a sounding board as we work to navigate our lives for ourselves. We appreciate that you were able to raise us into adulthood, but that is where your job ended and ours began. You will always be our mothers, but it is no longer your job to run our lives and give your perspective on how we should do things. Whether you realize it or not, this has been a major source of tension between us, as we have been trying to break free to discover life for ourselves. You have been holding on to us for dear life, smothering us in the process on our path toward growth and development. This has not helped us to become who we needed or wanted to be.

We ask that you release your role as our protective parent. We know that, in your heart, your intentions were only meant for our good. What we need now is for you to become our trusted advisor when things get too challenging for us to sort out on our own. Allow us to come to you first at the point we need. Typically, when we have received your unsolicited advice in the past, it has not helped us. Because of our desire to break free, it only helped to build further resentment in us toward you, as it felt like you were trying to control our every thought or action.

Today, we want to build bridges between us that bring us together, not separate us from each other. To do this, we are going to need your full participation with your open mind and open heart. Together, we can build a relationship that is based on mutual respect, trust, and love. This may include clear boundaries that will need to be respected. This will also require open and truthful dialogue between us. That dialogue at times may not be what you want to hear but these are our words coming from our hearts, so when you do not agree with them, we appreciate that you will try to see it from our perspective, not from the perspective of what you think is best for us.

Also, because we are not perfect beings, conflicts will arise in the future. All we ask when this happens is for you to be open to resolving the conflict instead of taking a hard stance on the subject. We hurt just as much as you do when we have unresolved conflict between us. Let's work together to ensure we do not let the sun go down on our anger with each other as scripture tells us in Ephesians 4:26. We know we need you in our lives, so we are willing to meet you in the middle, at the place where we can embrace each other in full, freely giving love. We will no longer guard our interactions with the hurtful words of the past that have kept us separated in our souls. Instead, we will be connected again as we once were in your loving womb.

We were created with parts of you strewn throughout our DNA, making us more like you than not. Just like God, we want to reflect you out in the world from a place of love, honor, and respect, and we are looking to you to help us get there.

We acknowledge our strained relationship has taken its toll on your heart, and for that, we are truly sorry. We acknowledge that at times you have probably felt like you were a failure and that you failed us. As we have grown into adults, we have learned—especially those of us who have become mothers—that this is the hardest job on the planet. Giving of yourself to ensure others can have a chance or opportunities to become who they dream of, at times means sacrificing your dreams and desires for the sake of your children. We realize that our harsh words and attitudes may have broken your spirit, sending you into silent tears wondering why we could be so cruel toward you when you were only trying to help. For this, we are so sorry!

Today, we are extending our hand out to you like we did when we were little girls, waiting for you to take hold of it and walk with us side by side on this journey. We desire to be reconnected spiritually, mentally, and physically with the person without whom we would not exist. We wish to restore the honor that is due to you for the courageous act of being the vessel of our existence through our thoughts, words, and actions toward you. Today, we come back to you humbled by the emptiness in our souls that we have been trying to fill with everything and anyone but you. We are humbled to admit the part we played through our puffed-up pride and resentment that did not serve us well or allow us to become the person we are destined by God's order to be because we did not acknowledge a key principle in God's world—to honor our mother. God will always humble His people and bring them to the truth. He does this so we can reconcile, restore, and live productive lives in joy, peace, and love.

Just like the Prodigal Son, we Prodigal Daughters also had to end up in the pig pen of our lives to get the message of reconnection. We thought you were someone we would live without but have learned that we cannot live the kind of life God has for us if we leave out our mothers. Please forgive us for all our painful words and actions, and most of all for the separation we created between us that made it uncomfortable for you to be near us, not knowing what to say or do in our presence. We cannot go back and change time, but we can open our minds and hearts to you as we move forward to rebuild our relationship with you and allow you to experience open love from us.

Thank you for being open to taking the time and energy to join us on this healing journey. Thank you for holding our hands through the process, drying the tears falling from our eyes, and clearing out years of old hurts and resentments to make room for love, laughter, and joy between us.

We believe as we are creating new memories, we will both reap many benefits. These benefits start with you helping us gain the ability to live a life free of regrets and obstacles that have held us back. We want the same for you too. Our heart's desire is to have a healed, mutually respectful relationship with you. We want there to be no hidden agendas or motives, nothing but a path of new truths we take and build together, starting today. We are looking forward, not rehashing the past, but healing our past to bring closure to what cannot be undone. We also believe that together we can rewrite our family history and, in our new relationship, become an example of a loving mother and daughter whose bond has the power to change this dynamic within our family for generations to come. Our prayer is simple: that we may experience the relationship God has always wanted for us as mother and daughter.

—Your loving daughters

Now, let's go to your Restoration Blueprint. Pull out your journal or companion guide. Let's start crafting your love letter to your mother. At the end of this exercise, the goal is for you to craft a very loving and honest letter to your mother in which you can feel confident about expressing what you have learned to her with the hope that this will start to facilitate a better relationship with her over time. Or you can use your letter as I did to start re-engaging your mother by living out what you expressed in your letter to her. The format for writing this letter will be in four parts, which are outlined next.

Part 1—This letter should open with your intention of love for your mother. I want you to acknowledge the past difficulties of this relationship and your present desire for it to change so that you can reconnect as mother and daughter, building a new relationship upon the foundation of mutual love and respect.

Part 2—In this section of the letter, describe how your past relationship with your mother shaped your thoughts, emotions, and actions to become who you are today. I want you to explain how this has been showing up in your life and affecting your other relationships, your career, and your spiritual belief in yourself. In this section, please make sure to indicate that you are not blaming her, just informing her of the impact on your life that resulted from being disconnected from her. Be sure to share with her how and why this is so important to you. She really needs to know this because it is possible that she may be thinking that having a relationship with you is something that could never happen. So do not make any assumptions about her thoughts or desire to have a relationship with you.

Part 3—Share the outcome you want to have with her and help her understand what reconnecting with her will mean to your healing journey and your relationship with her. Help her understand that this is a shared experience for the two of you as mother and daughter. Start to lay out the groundwork for what this repaired relationship could look like. Share some mother-daughter bonding experiences you would like to have with her. Let her know what these experiences would mean to you.

Part 4—Share with her all the benefits of your desired outcome for you, for her, for your family, and for generations to come. This will be a good time to show her how important she is in the equation of healing your family generationally. There is more on this in Chapter 9, "Generational Overrides."

Now it is time to write your own love letter to your mother. Find a space or place that brings you peace. It could be a place in your house that brings you peace, like a room with your favorite chair or a prayer room. It could also be an outdoor setting like a park or the beach. I want you to pick a place that is special to you. I want you to create a setting for yourself that allows you to open your heart and let the words flow out. Sometimes when you are in a setting that is too distracting, you will be in your head.

I want you to write this letter from your heartspace, not your headspace. For me, it's the beach. The sound of the waves crashing against the shore is very soothing and calming for me. The beach releases all my tension. It quiets my mind and opens my heart. Once you have done this, pick up your journal or companion guide, but don't open it yet. Just sit there with your journal or companion guide and think about all the notes you wrote as you have been going through this book. Smile at the place you are in today versus where you were when you first started this book. You have made great progress in revealing and reconstructing so far. Nice work, daughters! I am so proud of you. You are well on your way toward the restoration, reconciliation, and transformation of your relationship with your mother. You've got this!

It's time for this critical Restoration Blueprint exercise. Now, close your eyes and take a couple of deep breaths, lifting your shoulders as you inhale, then allowing them to fall as you exhale. Now open your journals or companion guides and begin your love letter, "Dear Mom…" and write powerfully! Once you have completed the letter, come back and finish this chapter.

Nice work, daughters! Wow! I am so excited for you. I know for some of you this was a very difficult experience, but you did it, so take a moment to smile at yourself again and say, "I did it!" Sit quietly for a moment and recognize this amazing step you took. Scary as it might have been, you nailed it!

I know the words you expressed in your letters were heart-centered and full of love and joy toward your mother. I pray that when she hears it, she will receive it from a place of openness, love, and appreciation. Did I say, "hears it?" Yes, I did. The next step in this process is to decide if you will deliver the letter to her in person or start living out your love letter in real time through your behaviors, words, and interactions with her. If you have decided to read her the letter, I want you to schedule some alone time with your mother and read the letter to her aloud. You will need to bring your journal, the book, and tissues to this engagement.

Pick a place to go with her that is not noisy or full of distractions. Try to create a quiet, peaceful setting like the one you created to write the letter if you can. I want the two of you to be in a private space where it is just the two of you alone as mother and daughter. At this meeting with your mother, I want you to begin the conversation by looking into your mother's eyes as you explain to her the journey you have been on through reading this book. The reason for this is that I want her to feel the genuineness of your words coming from your authentic self.

In this conversation, reveal to her your intention for reading this book and going through this process of healing. Let her know what it means to you and why it is so important to you. Give her space to process what you are saying. She may get tears in her eyes, but don't let this stop you. Allow her to process what she is hearing from you fully. Think about this: what if her tears are breaking down some of the walls she built up for protection because she never thought this moment would ever come? Sometimes she may be silent, and that's okay. Silence is a good thing. Allow the Holy Spirit to lead you through these moments. He will guide you when to speak and when to be silent. Tell her that you have written her a love letter you would like to read aloud to her.

Read her your letter, then take a moment of silence to let the words you have just read to her sink in. Often, we want to fill space with words to avoid silence because it feels uncomfortable. But silence is good for the soul and mind. In this silence, take some deep breaths and congratulate yourself for taking this giant step in the reconciliation process and for openly communicating your thoughts and feelings to your mother. This letter is going to open up more conversation with your mother. Sit back and talk with her. See where the conversation leads the both of you. Be mindful of emotions welling up for both of you.

For those who are taking this journey in real time, I want you to record your interaction in your journal or companion guide. Record how you felt and what you thought during the interactions and reflect on these feelings and thoughts. I also want you to record any victories you experience, from small to big, in your Restoration Blueprint. These are huge confidence builders in your relationship. They will also show you the progress you are making in your relationship. Also, note that at some point in the future, you may build up the courage to say verbatim what you wrote, which is also a huge confidence builder. I also encourage you to share with her that you are reading this book.

Regardless of the method you chose for delivering your love letter, I want you to invite your mother to join you for the remainder of your journey through this book. In Part 3, "Journey to Transformation," there are exercises and information that will help you build mutual respect, establish boundaries for engagement, and take steps to resolve conflict in healthy ways that will benefit both of you. As you move into Chapter 9, "Generational Overrides," you will also need her insight on the family patterns that have been developed over generations that were implanted in her and in you. Together, you can change the history of your family to have stronger connections by breaking some historical patterns. Again, I want to acknowledge your courage and let you know I am always praying for you and your mother. I am so excited to see what God does next in your relationship throughout the remainder of this book. Share your thoughts and experiences with me via my website at www.chequitamccullough.com.

CHAPTER 9

G is for Generational Overrides

The soul who sins shall die. The son shall not suffer for the iniquity of the father, nor the father suffer for the iniquity of the son. The righteousness of the righteous shall be upon himself, and the wickedness of the wicked shall be upon himself.

—Ezekiel 18:20, ESV

All my life, I have heard people—including myself and my family—say that we are under a generational curse. Our loving God does not bring curses upon us today. The ramifications and consequences of our choices under the free will God has gifted to us typically reveal the negative outcomes of our choices, but those outcomes are not curses. God wants us to live freed lives as individuals making sound and wise choices that lead to abundance in every area of our lives. This is why He sent Jesus to bear all our sins and remove all negative marks against us through the forgiveness of our sins with Jesus' death on the Cross. God is not holding what our parents, grandparents, or any other generation has done over our heads.

As we see above in Ezekiel 18:20, He treats everyone as individuals, holding them accountable for what they and they alone have done. We take our familial patterns and call them curses, dooming ourselves to struggle with overcoming obstacles. Then we turn them into badges of honor we must bear and wear because we were born into a family that has merely developed a history of repeating patterns from generation to generation. For me, it was the fear and anger I saw in my family. I thought that was supposed to be my destiny and legacy, but it was not. When I was a young adult, I fought very hard to not be what I saw or experienced in my family, only to acquiesce and become the very thing I did not want to be—an angry Black woman. The interesting thing I found out through therapy was that it really wasn't anger that was the problem, for me so much as it was the fear of living to my full potential. I was afraid to live for fear of failure. It came out as anger because living in fear was contradicting my heart's desire to be bold and fearless.

Familiar Familial Patterns

My mother shared a story about seeing her mother live a fearful life. She said my grandmother never stood up for herself, ever. She never did anything in life outside of the home where she raised her children. She used her home to hide from society and life. When we visited her house when I was young, she would not let us go outside and play because she did not want us to get hurt. My sister and I would stand at the window and look at other kids playing outside, but we were not allowed to join them. Even when our grandmother engaged with us, it was as though she was afraid of the youthful energy we exuded.

What struck me the most was that she always spoke in a whispered tone. It was like she was trying to shrink herself in the world, which is exactly what I did as a young adult. This was interesting because I did not spend that much time with my grandmother. But somewhere in our interactions, I had seen this behavior and adopted it unconsciously as a way to live. My mother, on the other hand, always vowed that she would not be like her mom, living small and full of fear. She did admit that she had just as much fear as her mother, but it came out loudly, in the form of anger and overprotection. Her perspective was that if she was loud, people would not think she had any fear. I became a blend of them both, fear and anger wrapped up as a combo package of destruction.

Familial patterns show up in all kinds of ways with people from all walks of life. Families have many years of patterns of teenage motherhood, alcoholism, obesity, criminal history, and mistreatment like verbal, sexual, and physical abuse. All these things did not happen to us because God wanted them to; they happened because of the learned patterns and experiences within our families and circumstances beyond our control. They are patterns that have not been broken by someone learning to do something different and passing on the new way to the next generations.

Breaking the Generational Pattern

It can take a lot to break the mold or pattern that has been in the family for generations. When you throw culture into it, it can become increasingly more difficult to break the family pattern. As I told people about this book, I often heard about patterns and cycles in other nationalities and cultures that had been repeated for generations. Even though we may be of a different race or nationality, we don't escape generational patterns. I tried unsuccessfully for decades to break the cycle of fear and anger. When you are too afraid to take chances in life for fear of failure, you end up living smaller than you were intended to. When you wake up in the morning mad for no reason, you discover you have a problem very easily. However, I never gave up. I continued to try until I broke the pattern for my family, which I could not have done without God's help and the help of therapists and many other people showing me different ways to live.

Another pattern my mother and I discussed was the rivalry between sisters, both her own and her mother's. My mother had aunts she never met because of their sister rivalry in her mother's circle. The constant arguing and bickering that ultimately led to hurt feelings and long periods of not speaking to or seeing each other also found its way into my relationship with my sister early in life and lasted until we reached our thirties. At that point, we decided together that we did not want to wake up old one day with a fractured relationship like we had seen between my mother and her three sisters all of our lives. We talked and talked about our past hurts, misunderstandings, and untruths.

How do I know the generational patterns are broken? Many ways. I no longer have a negative outlook on life, nor am I afraid to chase after my dreams, fearing failure as the outcome, as I did previously when I looked at my life through my very pessimistic eyes. I also see it in the way my son is raising his daughter. I see their engagement when she has done something that has disappointed him and how he handles that disappointment. He uses it as a learning opportunity to teach his daughter right from wrong rather than yelling at her in anger. I see it in my granddaughter's very healthy self-esteem and belief in herself. I can now see it in my son's healthy self-image, which he developed at a young age when I was still working to become a different type of mother than what I had experienced.

Patterns Kill the Soul

My sister and I made a choice to put in time and effort to repair what had previously been fractured. Now we are besties, telling each other everything and being champions of each other's successes, while also laughing at our human frailty together. We have developed a real sisterhood, breaking a generational pattern in our family.

Another thing that becomes a soul killer is when you experience or become the keeper of family secrets, whether by default or by being told to do so. When I was growing up, in the Black culture, it was a spoken and unspoken rule that you never talked about what went on inside of your house. You were instructed to paint a picture that was not necessarily reality. You then had to perpetuate that lie day in and day out to keep up the front and not expose the family's secrets. You never did or said anything that would bring shame on your family. We have also been taught to hide and run from problems, but not how to solve them. Before it was culturally acceptable to walk away from critical relationships as it is today, we as a culture had mastered the ghosting technique. We have seen many family members ousted, making us think this was an acceptable practice. This allowed us to discard our relationships with our mothers without blinking an eye or losing any sleep, or so we told ourselves. However, it is not the right thing to do, spiritually or otherwise.

Here is an example of how secrets and lies can impact a family. In my own family, relatives have become sick with diseases and died. Prior to their death, however, the person was portrayed as having a clean bill of health. Then suddenly they would die for apparently no reason. The lie was that they died suddenly for no reason, but the truth was that they died because they did not seek medical treatment that could have saved their life. Ridiculous! Did it ever occur to anyone that the diseases other members of our families experienced might also affect us too at some point in the future? When we know what exists within the family, we can seek medical treatment or preventive measures and not succumb to the same fate.

I remember when my grandfather died, someone commented that I wasn't crying. As I think about it now, I don't know why I didn't cry. Could it have been because I didn't know which man I was supposed to grieve—the secret one who was abusive to his family or the one I knew and loved? Secrets and lies hurt our souls. I am not saying that you need to shout what happens in your family or to you from the mountain top. What I am saying is that secrets and lies are very destructive behaviors that, when not dealt with properly, can do a lot of damage. In my opinion, this is where mental health specialists come into play to help people process and deal with secrets and lies in a healthy way, so they do not become destructive, especially with children.

Cultural Secrets and Shame

The secrets in the Black community have been killing the souls of our daughters for generations. Unforgiveness, anger, resentment, and denial can be seen everywhere. Nothing for me is more disappointing than to see this play out on the TV airwaves where we show the ugliest of the ugly to the world. Fighting each other in public, playing to the stereotype of the angry Black woman for the world to see, is not a true representation of us at all. We are beautiful, bold, courageous, smart, unique, sexy, dynamic, multifaceted, and multitalented. This is what gets displayed on the airwaves about us probably only 20 percent of the time, as opposed to 80 percent of the ugly. It literally at times makes me cry and scream. Our secrets have been kept since slavery, invading our souls, making us feel unworthy of love and respect, and showing us that we are only worthy of abuse, pain, and suffering, both silently and publicly.

Even though slavery has long been over, those scars have unfortunately been carried forward through our generational lineage. Do we have a right to be angry about these scars? Yes. Should we try to break those chains and bonds for our girls after all this time? Yes. I am hopeful today; I see my Black sisters rising up everywhere to break these chains in positive ways, showing our girls new possibilities. We need to continue to heal ourselves and each other until there is little to no trace of our painful pasts reflected in our bright futures. I do not want to walk down another sidewalk and have my Black sisters not acknowledge my presence. I want to see us acknowledging that we see each other with loving smiles and nods of appreciation. I want to see us validating each other and recognizing that we are all worthy.

I know some of you reading this book had to keep far worse secrets than mine. I know those secrets are hard truths that some people have had to carry around for a long time. I remember in high school a girl got pregnant. You could see her belly growing but the lie that was fabricated and told by the school administration until she left school was that she had a tumor in her belly. I always felt so bad for her because becoming pregnant in high school is not a fate any young girl wants to face intentionally. Back then, girls who got pregnant in school were also ushered out because they would be considered a bad influence on the remainder of us girls at school, as though we might get the idea to get pregnant too from seeing a pregnant girl every day at school. Ridiculous, but true. That poor girl may still be dealing with the effects of perpetuating that fabricated story but hopefully, she has grown stronger despite it. How was this even remotely helpful to her or the other girls in our school?

Altered Realities

What did this lie teach us? It taught us to pretend we do not know how to distinguish falsehood from reality. It taught us to create a false narrative of what our life really is. It taught us how to distort reality and make up something that became our truth when we were faced with our own indiscretions or a reality that was less than perfect. This is how we got to some of the narratives we have in our minds about our mother-daughter relationships and what they were versus what they might have been. We have lived our lives somewhere in between truth and fiction because we were taught to. Today, we see this all over social media—postings of only the good but nothing about reality, showing the good but not the bad.

I want to help us start to live from our authentic truth instead of from a fabricated and distorted reality. Whether or not we want to admit it, we can plant and might have already planted some of these seeds in our children, especially our girls. Do we really want our girls to grow up living a distorted version of the truth? I am working to give my granddaughter all the benefits of life that support her in becoming her best authentic self early on. When she was born, I was at first a little gun-shy about this beautiful baby girl simply because of my old fear that my experiences meant I would mess up a girl child.

Even though I had done my work and was living differently, I still had that fear in the back of my mind. My heart, however, took over and fell in love with her, and I committed to making sure she was and is nurtured in all the ways I longed to be when I was her age.

I have seen myself in her as she has grown from an infant to a young girl, and so has my family, who are constantly telling me she acts just like I did when I was her age. My words are always affirming her, my answers to her questions are always truthful, and my engagement with her is all about making sure she is growing and developing in ways that support where she is now and where she will be going in the future.

The Rewards of Broken Patterns

What I am most proud of is that she gets to experience a much better, more authentic version of me than my son did at her age. I at times feel like God has given me another shot to get some things right with my granddaughter that I was not fully equipped to do when I was raising my son. I now get to help him raise a healthy young girl. What she knows for sure is that I will move heaven and earth to ensure she gets whatever she needs, and I will not allow her soul to be affected in the ways mine was at that young age.

Jesus died for us to live a freed life, which includes freedom from familial or generational patterns. I love what the Bible says in 1 Peter 2:16 (ESV): "Live as people who are free, not using your freedom as a cover-up for evil, but living as servants of God." God's intention is right there, "not using your freedom as a cover-up!" One of the most loving things we can do is to help our families fight through these familiar familial patterns for change. It only takes one person going against the grain to move the direction of an entire family. We have seen that many times throughout the Bible when we look at a few who did this, like Abraham, Noah, and Moses. They all moved in the direction of change that God was calling them to and changed the course of history for their entire families, and in the case of Moses, the entire nation of Israel, which started with his mother and sister, Jochebed and Miriam.

That same power of change resides within us too. In fact, Ephesians 3:12 (ESV) tells us that "we have boldness and access with confidence through our faith in Him." We can use this faith and confidence to help our families gain freedom. It must start somewhere with someone; why not you? We are overriding the generational patterns and writing new patterns to set up our families for success now and in the future. I am calling on you daughters to start and facilitate this change. Be mindful that you might get some resistance. Change is not easy for everybody. Change also takes time. It is almost like a chipping-away process over time.

At some point, a conversation with your mother will need to take place. As women, we are often placed in the position of keeping someone's secret. This will in some cases require delicate conversations. Again, the intention is not to be a bull in a China shop, demanding all the secrets be given up. The intention is to find out what the secrets are and how they have been impacting the family generationally so they can start to be exposed and broken apart. Then the healing process can begin for current and future generational change.

Here are some of the generational statements I have heard from family and friends over the years.

- I'm like this because my mother was like this; this is just how the women in my family are.
- No one in my family has ever amounted to anything, and I won't either.

- My family has high blood pressure and diabetes, so I'm going to have it too.
- We are poor, and we are always going to be poor.
- Girls do not get opportunities; those are reserved for the boys in the family.

My question to you is this: are you going to live under the generational umbrella of untruths or are you going to use the individuality God gave you to forge your own path?

Reframing the generational talk . . .

- I may have some of my mother's ways but that does not mean I have to follow her path.
- Just because I do not see a picture of success in my family does not mean I cannot become successful.
- Just because my family has health issues does not mean I have to follow them. I can live a healthier lifestyle to help mitigate what I may be predisposed to from my family.
- If I educate myself and work hard, I do not have to repeat the pattern of poverty.

Time to add to your Restoration Blueprint. For this journaling exercise, I want to you write out all the patterns you have seen or experienced in your family. For each one, ask this question: How am I going to change this pattern for me and my family? This is a great exercise to do with your mother, your daughters, and any other female family members. Covering multiple generations will help to bring out the familial patterns that have been developed. When you can identify them, then they can be changed within your family for future generations. Working together as a collaborative unit is a great opportunity to mend and heal generational patterns. I pray this exercise will be extremely fruitful for you, your mother, and your family, and that you help bring your family into a new light. Scripture says, "for at one time you were in darkness, but now you are the light in the Lord. Walk as children of light." (Ephesians 5:8, ESV)

As this chapter ends, take note that the image on the next page depicts all of the pieces of the heart put back together through the *HEALING* journey. You have built a heart of hope, one that can see and have new experiences that serve you well. You should be proud of yourself for walking through this journey despite feeling fear or reservation. You are not the same person you were when you started this journey.

A Heart of Hope

The journey to a healed heart does not stop at the end of this book. It is a lifelong journey. We are only fully healed when we get to heaven. This book offers a new way of being in a relationship with your mother in which you have both reconciled with the past relationship and are ready to begin a new relationship with a clean slate. Now that this process has been started, it invites you to reconnect with your mother with a new mindset, a new heartset, and new tools to engage her from a position that empowers you in healthy ways, whether or not she has changed. The image above of the puzzle pieces forming the whole heart is a visualization that symbolizes the work you have put in on this HEALING journey to start the reconciliation and reconstruction moving forward toward that new relationship.

Scripture says, "So now faith, hope, and love abide, these three; but the greatest of these is love." (1 Corinthians 13:13, ESV) Throughout the process of this book, you have held onto your faith and had tremendous hope that grew in love, not only toward your mother but also for yourself. Because you did not give up, you gained a clearer picture that has led to more confidence, strength, perseverance, patience, and wisdom. All these attributes are also attributes of God, which means you have become more like Him through this process. When you look in the mirror now, what do you see? Do you even recognize yourself? I will venture to say that you do not even recognize who you have become. This much better version of who you are is also noticed by others in your circle, whether they be friends or family. I told you at the beginning of this book that this experience would be transformational if you allowed it to be. I am so proud of you for staying the course on this important journey. My heart is filled with so much joy because you allowed me to walk with you through your HEALING journey. Because I know the journey you have undertaken, I know your future will be brighter than you even know. May your steps continue to be blessed and filled with joy as you continue to reconnect with your mother. Know that God is also pleased because another mother-daughter relationship has been restored.

Part 3

Journey to Transform

Behold, I will bring to it health and healing, and I will heal them and reveal to them abundance of prosperity and security.

—Jeremiah 33:6, ESV

A Prayer of Transformation

Jehovah-Rapha,

God of healing and transformation, it is Your desire that all of your people be healed, which is why You sent Your Son to bear all iniquities and heal all.

Your glorious power brings healing to all who believe in Your Son, Jesus Christ.

Your promise of healing not only restores our souls but adds additional transformative values like abundance, prosperity, and security to all facets of our lives.

Lord God, there are so many abundant blessings given to us when we are healed.

We can love more, we can praise more, we can be who you have created us to be as whole and healed beings created for good in the world. Proverbs 17:22 tells us that a joyful heart is good medicine.

Thank you for stretching out Your hand to heal us, showing us the signs and wonders to come for us with the healing of our relationships with our mothers.

We look forward to experiencing the love and joy of this relationship and being a model for others, but also being a testament of Your glory that shows the prosperity and security of healed relationships uniting one another in love.

We honor and bless Your holy name for this healing of every part of us that was broken.

In Jesus' mighty name. Amen!

CHAPTER 10

Facilitating and Expanding God's Love

If anyone says, "I love God," and hates his brother, he is a liar; for he who does not love his brother whom he has seen cannot love God whom he has not seen. And this commandment we have from him: whoever loves God must also love his brother.

—1 John 4:20-21, ESV

And above all these put on love, which binds everything together in perfect harmony.

—Colossians 3:14, ESV

Hello, Daughters!

I am so proud of you. You have stayed the course and processed a lot of heartfelt emotions through the previous chapters. Some of you have gone on a rollercoaster ride of emotions, taking you up and down and back up again. You are growing in love with yourselves and the accomplishments and strides you have made on this journey. I never said it was going to be easy, but it is most definitely necessary for you to rebuild the relationship you want with your mother. You would not have been able to get here had you not gone through the process of healing your soul from the inside out. For each one of you, this process is very different. This is not a cookie-cutter process. God was not using a cookie-cutter process when He made you. Your individuality plays a huge part in your healing process, so do not compare your journey to anyone else's.

This healing journey is yours and yours alone. Others will get the benefit of your healing, but no one can take credit for it. What you will be doing from here on out is growing in love, becoming facilitators of love, and expanding God's kingdom through your loving thoughts, words, and actions. When you grow in love, you are no longer bound to your past hurts, replaying those hurts over and over in your heads or acting them out loud at the most inopportune times. You have prayed, gotten help, and done the lessons in this book to process your way through the healing. You are prepared to do things differently from here on out. Will you be perfect? I hope not! There is no growth in perfection; you only grow when you make a mistake or misstep. God is not expecting you to be perfect. He only expects you to be human in a real, authentic, human experience, figuring things out every day.

Lessons On Love

Let's look at the two scriptures that opened this chapter for a moment. As Christians, we love to let everyone in our space know that we love God, as we confess it with our mouths. However, I want you to understand what loving God means. 1 John 4:20-21 tells us that we cannot say we love God and hate, dislike, or not care for another person. We cannot split God's principles in half and only accept a portion of the principle. We must love ourselves and everyone regardless of circumstances. We do not have to love what they may have done but we do need to love the person simply because they are one of God's children. Will this be difficult to accomplish? Only if we allow it to be by holding onto unforgiveness. As I talked about earlier in this book, I had to look beyond what my mother had done or said to be able to look at her through the eyes of love. That is what God's principle is telling us to do. We are to look beyond what we see and love anyway. We love Him and we have never seen Him, which shows us that we can do it. Now we have a choice to make to do it with the people around us like our mothers.

We see in Colossians 3:14 that we are to "put on love" which binds all things in "perfect harmony." Love brings harmony. Love brings order. Love brings restoration. Love brings reconciliation. Love brings transformation. Love brings unity. Love brings love. Where there is love there cannot be discord. Where there is love there cannot be hate. Where there is love there is no separation. The reason God sent Jesus to Earth was to provide the ultimate reconciliation and restoration of us back to Himself. This brought us back into harmony with Him through His love for us.

Love Is Action

What facilitates God's love? We do. How do we facilitate this love? When we start with self-love, and then show others love through our words and actions.

Before you can love another human being fully, you must first learn to love yourself fully. When you love yourself fully, this is when you start to show up in the world as your authentic, loving self. You get to self-love by surrendering yourself to God in prayer and meditation and allowing Him to show you the places you need to improve to become your most authentic self. Being your authentic self is your empowerment because you are no longer pretending to be someone you are not. You are showing up in the world fully present for people to see you, flaws and all.

Authenticity comes through your self-love so you can walk in freedom and appreciation with your head held high. Self-love is letting go of your hurts and not holding on to them, hiding yourself from the world. You have been wearing these hurts around your neck like beads of a wooden necklace, each bead representing a hurt that someone inflicted upon you. It's time to cut this necklace off your neck so you can lift your head up confidently, living free within yourself from the burden of these hurts so you can embrace a freed mindset and accept the love that Jesus Christ died to give you.

Self-love is the key for you to conform to the image of Christ. Self-love allows you to look in a mirror and appreciate what you see reflected back to you. This is the love of Christ that is in us now, reflecting outward so that when you see this reflection, you are not criticizing what you see but are instead loving it. You are so beautiful, inside and out. You have finally come to a place in your life where the inner and outer beauty are in unison and have become one within. I think you should give God some praise right here! You made it! You have surrendered and accepted self-love. When you look in the mirror, you actually like what you see. You can see love through your own eyes when you look out into the world. When you engage with others with your eyes and soul filled with love, this is how you facilitate God's love.

Now, how do you expand God's love? This is done when you go back to reconcile and restore your relationships through love, starting with your mother. Congratulations to you for taking the very brave steps necessary to start expanding God's love earlier in the process. I pray you are learning and growing in love as a result.

For those of you who have not yet taken that first very scary step to start to bridge this gap, do not worry. You are right where you need to be in the process. Believe me, I know how scary it is to take steps in this direction, especially when you have tried and failed in the past. As you begin to plan out what the steps of engagement with your mother might look like, remember this: each of us is different so this can look a number of different ways because there is not a one-way-fits-all approach for re-engagement from your new, empowered state. For example, I chose an over-the-phone approach because I do not live close to my mom, and I did not want to wait until I saw her on a special occasion like the holidays.

Here are some things to keep in mind as you select your approach. Whenever people are getting together in celebration of something or for a family gathering, it is probably not the best time to try to bridge the gap with your mother. As we have discussed previously, the mother-daughter relationship is one of the most complex relationships to navigate. It is not fair to your family members to try to fix this before a celebratory event because the reconciliation process could get off to a rocky start and therefore negatively impact the family gathering.

Also, this should be something that takes place between you and your mother alone first before letting the family into your private time. The reason for this is family has their own perspective on your relationship with your mother. They may not understand the work you have put in to get to this place and will, out of the goodness of their hearts, advise you to leave well enough alone. Thank and bless them but remember this is something you want to do because you are trying to get to a place of full healing and restoration for both of you.

Believe me, as you and your mother start to work together—understanding each other, processing the hurts, and moving to a place where you are ready to communicate—others will notice. They will notice when the tension is no longer there when the two of you are in proximity to each other. They will notice when they see you and your mother engaging with one another in loving ways. Reconciliation is a powerful thing. It is a catalyst for seeing real transformation for us and through us if we allow it.

A Loving Approach

Let's figure out an approach you might take for future conversations. If you have not sat with your mother and read your Letter of Reconciliation, then set up a time to do it. Remember that the goal of the letter is to be the starting point for reconnection between the two of you. If you have already sat with your mother and read her your beautifully crafted Letter of Reconciliation from Chapter 8, then you can move forward to take more steps that could be useful in formulating a new relationship going forward. You will need to think in detail about your intentions and the goal you want to achieve as you move forward. You will first need to get very clear on your intention.

The goal is to reconnect with your mother on a deeper level, on the level that you always desired in your heart and dreamed about in your mind. You have a trifecta of love on our side in God, Jesus, and the Holy Spirit to lead you through this important exercise. You will never lose at life when you are pushing through your fears, seeking love in the name of expanding God's love. God is watching you; the

Holy Spirit is helping you, and Jesus has already shown you how to do it through His many examples within the Bible. Be bold and brave through this exercise because you are equipped to be and do.

Before you move into the next journaling Restoration Blueprint exercise, I want you to spend some time visualizing your future relationship with your mother. I want you to get the picture in your mind of how you see the two of you engaging now as you rebuild your relationship.

- Take a few deep breaths to clear your energy and relax your body.
- Close your eyes and take a few more breaths.
- Imagine feeling the smile on your face when you see her.
- Imagine you see a smile on her face when she sees you.
- Imagine what your mother's arms feel like around you as she gives you a loving embrace.
- Imagine feeling yourself melting into her embrace.
- Imagine her hands caressing your beautiful face as she looks into your eyes.
- Imagine hearing her say the words, "I love you."

Then open your eyes when you are ready and take this loving energy into the journaling session as you answer the questions in the next exercise. Doesn't this feel amazing? It is possible to achieve and become a reality in your future. I am praying for this to happen for you and your mother in your near future.

HEALING

Below are a few prompting questions to ask yourself as you journal, adding to your Restoration Blueprint in preparation for your next scheduled meeting with your mother. These questions are important because they can be the framework for you to use to start and continue bridging the gap between the two of you. Do not placate yourself with surface-level answers when answering these questions. You have come too far and done too much work to simply scratch the surface in this exercise. So, speak the truth in love to yourself as you go through these questions. When you dive into the truth, you are blessed with much better outcomes and, in some cases, miracles. I encourage you to pray, meditate, and add additional questions of your own that will help to make this experience more personal.

- Why is reconciling with your mother important to you?
- How are you going to approach your mother about rebuilding your relationship with her? In person, over the phone, video call, or in a heartfelt letter?
- What do you hope to gain from the restored relationship?
- What do you hope she gains from your restored relationship?
- What do you want this relationship to look like as it moves forward?

- What can you compromise on to get to your ideal relationship?
- What are you not able to compromise on?
- What are you willing to do to ensure that the lines of communication remain open between the two of you?
- Name three things you are willing to do to continue showing respect, love, and commitment to rebuilding this relationship. These three things are to be shared with your mother for accountability in your relationship with her.

I highly encourage you to share these questions and answers with your mother. They can be good conversation pieces between the two of you. They can also show her that you are serious about rebuilding your relationship, and they can possibly be the conduit that opens her up to seeing things differently between the two of you. You will be surprised when you share your information with her, how she softens to the possibilities of something better between the two of you. These types of questions and moments create opportunities to grow your relationship for the better have far-reaching benefits, more than you even know.

Remember, my intention was very clear. I wanted to be able to be fully present with my mother on her deathbed and express my gratitude and love for her with no regrets. This was the foundation on which I built my reconciliation plan. From this intention, I was able to build my reconciliation plan. Once I started the conversation, I also incorporated a very key element—a real curiosity to know my mother so I could come to understand the path she had walked before she became pregnant with me. I wanted to know about her perspective on life as an eight-year-old girl, a teenager, and a young woman. I wanted to know what she dreamt of becoming when she grew up. I wanted to know what dreams she had for me when I was still inside of her womb. Thinking about these things also took the focus off me and kept it on us.

Love Is Intentional

On the flip side, I had to help my mother come to know who her daughter had grown up to be because I had kept almost my entire life from her. She only knew what she could see during the limited times we engaged with one another. As a result, her view of me was distorted and based on old data or an outdated lens. She only knew what I wanted her to see all those years ago.

In the next chapter, you will build the final phase of the Restoration Blueprint to rebuild your relationship and expand the love between the two of you by using clearly formatted exercises to build mutual respect and boundaries, as well as work with conflict resolution tools. These will be great journaling exercises for your Restoration Blueprint as you and your mother work together to rebuild your relationship based on mutual respect and love for one another. I am still praying for the growth and development of your new relationship. In these exercises, you will write out your answers to the questions as individuals and then come together to discuss your answers. This is how the reconciliation bridge begins as you each read your answers and discuss them together.

Intentionally working together as a mother-daughter duo is the goal of the next chapter. As you are setting the framework for your relationship together, it may be a little clunky at first because you are still learning to work together to build respect and boundaries, as well as learning how to manage conflict. That's okay. Starting something new always feels a little clunky at first, but in time it gets better. You've got this!

CHAPTER 11

God's Perspective on
Reconciliation and Restoration

. . . that God was reconciling the world to himself in Christ, not counting people's sins against them. And he has committed to us the message of reconciliation. We are therefore Christ's ambassadors, as though God were making his appeal through us. We implore you on Christ's behalf: Be reconciled to God.

—2 Corinthians 5:19-20, NIV

God highly values reconciliation and restoration. We know this because He used Jesus to reconcile and restore the whole world, including our relationships, back to Himself. Reconciliation and restoration are two more key principles in Christian living, but also for all of humanity, no matter what one's beliefs are. We were all created to be in relationships. Those relationships are meant to be healthy ones. Even when we don't have healthy relationships, we should work to create and facilitate them. Restoration is God's endgame, which means it should be ours too.

What I love about studying God's Word is that when you really study His intention and purpose, you learn the value of what He offers us. He always gives us a promise, and in these promises, we get to experience great benefits in our lives for embracing His principles. As I studied many scriptures on restoration, I saw a theme that when we restore what is important to God, we are restored with a minimum of double of something good like hope, faith, joy, strength, possessions, and so many other things that are added back to us. How will He bless us for restoring our relationships with our mothers? So far, I have received inner peace, joy, laughter, and courage, as well as a greater appreciation, respect, and love for my mother. And I continue to be surprised by the unexpected.

Remember what Isaiah shared with us: "Instead of your shame there shall be a double portion; instead of dishonor they shall rejoice in their lot; therefore in their land they shall possess a double portion; they shall have everlasting joy." (Isaiah 61:7, ESV) As you move forward to reconcile and restore your relationship with your mother, you should expect to receive these promises from God. When you restore your relationships, you also release your internal shame and move to a place of forgiveness, allowing you to honor your mother. In honor, there is peace, love, joy, reconciliation, and restoration of your soul.

Respect, Boundaries, and Conflict Resolution

For you to get to reconciliation and restoration in your relationship with your mother, you need to set up guidelines for this new relationship. These three key elements will help you rebuild the foundation for a solid relationship that can continue to grow and develop in the future. These three elements are: Respect, Boundaries, and Conflict Resolution.

Mutual Respect

Respect is the first key to success for any relationship. Without respect for yourself and for your mother, nothing will change. Most of us think respect is earned, and it is to a certain degree. In past chapters, I talked about responsibility and accountability. Thinking back on your interactions with your mother, can you honestly and truthfully say you were respectful and justifiable? Jesus confronted the men who wanted to stone the woman who committed infidelity because, though her actions were not right, stoning her was also not justifiable.

Given this new perspective, let's continue to talk about building respect toward your mother. The biblical benefit of gaining respect for your mother is that when you "Love each other with genuine affection, and take delight in honoring each other" (Romans 12:10, NLT), your relationship can start to grow. Another benefit of respecting your mother is that it opens the door for you to build up your feelings of trust. When you can rebuild your feeling of trust toward her, eventually you can learn to feel safe with her. When you feel safe, your heart begins to soften, forgiveness starts to be given freely, and your soul can begin to heal.

Trust also leads you to become a better listener in this new relationship, as you will no longer be listening from a position of defensiveness but of curiosity to learn what your mother has to say. The benefit is that you are building open lines of communication, something some of us have never had. Imagine this for a moment: an open line of communication with your mother—not a guarded line of communication, but an open one. Isn't that powerful to think about? This is why Respect is one of the stones in the new foundation. The first stone, as you learned in the previous chapter, is Love.

Defining Boundaries

The next stone in the new foundation is Boundaries. These boundaries are not barriers intended to keep people at a distance. They are guidelines to help people understand how to engage with you, which is actually a benefit to both parties. As I looked for a biblical representation of boundaries, I landed on 2 Corinthians 8:13-14 in the New Living Translation, which says:

> Of course, I don't mean your giving should make life easy for others and hard for yourselves. I only mean that there should be some equality. Right now, you have plenty and can help those who are in need. Later, they will have plenty and can share with you when you need it. In this way, things will be equal.

These verses are a call to generous giving, but when I read them, I also saw that the principle of equality could be applied when setting boundaries for your new relationship with your mother.

Verse 13 says "our giving should not make life easy for others and hard for ourselves." Applying this principle to setting boundaries, you do not want to make the path of boundaries rigid out of fear from your past. Both sides should set boundaries to get to common ground that is mutually beneficial for mother and daughter. As you begin to forge your new relationship, remember that throughout this book you have gained some new tools and therefore you are more prepared to begin this new relationship than your mother may be. As you set your boundaries, set them from a place of fairness so that in the future, the relationship for both can be one of giving and receiving—an equal exchange. If these boundaries for engagement are so rigid that they become uncomfortable for both mother and daughter, this will defeat the purpose of having boundaries.

You are trying to get to the place where you are opening doors and lines of communication. While you might like to believe that once the lines of communication are reopened, everything is going to be perfect between you and your mother, it is not. And that is where boundaries come into play. Remember at the beginning of the book I said you would be rebuilding your relationship? Boundaries are necessary in all types of relationships. Do not misinterpret this as building more walls around you. You are not doing that. You are providing your mother with guidelines that will help her navigate her new relationship with you.

Without boundaries, you are likely to end up in a relationship that is not healthy for you. With your mother, that could mean you end up back where you started, in a fractured relationship with no peace. Keep in mind that setting boundaries is not a punitive action; it is a loving action. It is loving because you are telling people how to engage with you in a way that will be a positive experience for both you and them. Also, when people understand your boundaries, they are in a more relaxed state in your presence, as you are in theirs. When you are made to feel like you are walking on eggshells or waiting for a bomb to drop, this is because there are no boundaries for the engagement.

Biblical Conflict Resolution

The last stone in this foundation is Conflict Resolution. One of the best biblical lessons for conflict resolution is the entirety of Matthew Chapter 7 (ESV), but you are going to lean into God's Golden Rule, outlined in verses 12 through 14:

So whatever you wish that others would do to you, do also to them, for this is the Law and the Prophets. Enter by the narrow gate. For the gate is wide and the way is easy that leads to destruction, and those who enter by it are many. For the gate is narrow and the way is hard that leads to life, and those who find it are few.

This scripture is very clear that when you do not resolve conflict, it only leads to destruction, in relationships with others as well as within yourself. Hurt feelings, stress, anxiety, and anger are all very destructive emotions that not only take a mental toll but also a physical one as well. It is critical that you learn to resolve conflict so that you can remain healthy, both mentally and physically. This is very important to keep in mind as you move forward.

Conflicts can be big or small, so understanding how to navigate conflict resolution in both extremes will help you in the long run. Why do you need to know how to resolve conflict? Because, as human beings, we will always have conflict. I would venture to say that, for most of you reading this book, the conflicts with your mother started before you were really emotionally developed and, if you are being truthful, some of you are still emotionally underdeveloped and therefore not equipped to handle conflict in a healthy manner. Trying to resolve conflict from an underdeveloped emotional state only leads to hurt feelings within yourself and others.

As a coach, I help people learn to manage their emotions in healthy ways. Emotions are necessary and needed in life. They can either work for you or against you. In your relationship with your mother, they have often worked against you. Part of successful conflict resolution is the ability to manage your emotions during conflict. When you are in an emotionally charged state, you do not have the ability to see the situation clearly or find solutions to bring the conflict to a close. An example is when you are in a highly charged argument with someone with words flying back and forth, some of those words are hurtful on both sides. After you have retreated to your respective corners and cooled down, you often cannot remember half of the things that were said, but you do remember the emotional hurt caused by some of those words.

An analogy I like to use for emotions is a hurricane. We all know that at the center of a hurricane, or the eye, it is calm and peaceful, but everything outside of the eye is swirling around at a dizzying pace. The outer bands of the hurricane are your emotions when you are in conflict. You are trying to get to the eye of the hurricane where it is peaceful, often without any tools to help you get there. You are trying to bring resolution in the bands of the hurricane where it is chaotic, instead of the eye where you can clearly see what is going on around you from a place of peace.

I have developed a few exercises that can help you build tools to get and give respect, set clear boundaries, and learn to respect the boundaries of others, as well as manage your emotions in times of conflict so that you can effectively resolve conflict when it arises. It's time to get out your journal or companion guide and add to your Restoration Blueprint to continue building on your notes for the discussion with your mother.

You cannot open the lines of communication without a definitive plan of action. These exercises are three critical steps for building a solid foundation for the new relationship. When you add communication to the cornerstone pieces of love, respect, boundaries, and conflict resolution, you have a solid foundation to move forward with more success in this relationship. In the next exercise, you are first going to build this blueprint from your perspective. As you start to re-engage your mother from your new, enlightened position of restoration and reconciliation, I would like you to give this exercise to her so that she can formulate what this might look like for her. Once this is completed, you both can discuss your blueprints together and thus start the rebuilding process with a foundation of understanding that is mutually beneficial for the future growth and development of your relationship.

Restoration Blueprint
Building Respect Exercise

Respect questions for you

What does respect mean to you?

What does respect look like to you?

What do you think respect looks like to your mother?

When you feel respected, what does that look like?

When you feel disrespected, what does that look like?

What does it look like when you are giving respect to yourself?

What does it look like when you are giving respect to others?

What can respect look like when you are extending it to your mother?

Respect questions for your mother

What does respect mean to you?

What does respect look like to you?

What do you think respect looks like to your daughter?

When you feel respected, what does that look like?

When you feel disrespected, what does that look like?

What does it look like when you are giving respect to yourself?

What does it look like when you are giving respect to others?

What can respect look like when you are extending it to your daughter?

Once you and your mother have both completed your answers, review them together. The goal here is to come to a mutually beneficial agreement wherein both of you feel comfortable with your plan of action to maintain respect in your interactions and engagements. I would highly recommend that you also build mechanisms so that if respect is broken, you will both honor the consequence of the broken respect. Tools to build this section of the exercise will come under the Conflict Resolution portion later in this chapter. Now let's move into exercise #2, Building Healthy Boundaries.

Restoration Blueprint
Building Healthy Boundaries

First, let's understand that the boundaries you are defining are mutual boundaries for you and your mother. You can only control setting the boundaries you want; you cannot control the other person's boundaries. Be careful when explaining boundaries, as they can be perceived to keep someone at a distance. That is not what we are doing in this exercise. In setting the boundaries together with your mother, the goal is to come to an understanding that these boundaries are in place to help us have successful engagement and build a meaningful relationship that supports both of you.

"No" is a Loving Word

A key word in setting your boundaries is "no." This word will be the place most people get tripped up because of the way it is used versus what you are trying to convey. I often tell my family and friends that the word "no" does not require an explanation, nor does it require an apology to be used in conjunction with it.

If I do not want to do something that is asked of me, why do I need to cover the word "no" in an explanation? "No" simply means no to whatever the request may be. It is as simple as that.

The use of the word "no" in a relationship will also mean that there will be times when you too have to accept it without explanation or apology from someone else. When used appropriately, the word "no" can be a powerful tool. Most often, those who do not have a healthy boundary of their own will be offended by the word.

Another boundary is that you are not responsible for how people receive your "no." Your "no" has to stand on its own as a given boundary. The feelings of others and their emotions regarding your "no" have no bearing on your decision to use the word. You should not feel guilty or responsible for another person's feelings when you use the word "no." This is something the other person will need to process on their own and come to accept, or not.

This simple word often brings tension in relationships because one or both parties use it as a tool to hurt the other person versus a tool to set healthy boundaries. If you get mad when you hear the word "no," a good way to check in with yourself is to simply ask yourself the question, "Why is this word producing this negative emotion?" Most likely, it is an old pattern you have developed that needs to be examined and reframed as a boundary-setting tool instead.

Safeguard and Flexibility

Boundaries should be flexible because, as you grow in respect, trust, and ability to resolve conflict in a healthy way, your boundaries will change. There can always be safeguards for you, but they no longer need to be fortresses you build around yourself for protection if you are trying to rebuild a relationship with your mother. Being in a relationship with your mother means you are trying to make a connection with her. In doing so, you are working to get to a state of openness that requires flexibility on your part.

A word of caution here: some of your boundaries might still be connected to the emotions that lead you to judge interactions or words from your mother more harshly. Be mindful of this and remember that some of the work you have done throughout this book may no longer need a boundary, but if your frame of reference is tied to old experiences, you will need to look at these emotions through your new lens that is focused on where you want to get in your relationship with your mother.

Building Healthy Boundaries Exercise

Before you outline the boundaries that are important to you—such as emotional, physical, tone of voice, words, and physical gestures—let's get clear about when boundaries have been broken in the past and how they were broken. Open your journal or companion guide and write out statements about how each of these areas was used by your mother in the past. The reason for this exercise is to see how these areas might affect your ability to openly engage with your mother now. Even though you worked on forgiveness in a past chapter, your emotions and experiences have been wrapped up and bound tightly together for years. You are slowly going through the unraveling process to uncover what is underneath the intertwined mess that had a grip on you all this time. You are trying to bring things to light that may hinder you as you work to move forward in your relationship with your mother. Here are some examples of what to look for as you process through your thoughts and experiences.

- Tone of voice—high pitched, snarky, condescending, judgmental, highly critical
- Spoken words—yelling, sarcasm, offhanded comments, comments through other people
- A created period of silence and/or space between the two of you
- Physical gestures such as smirks, eye rolls, a crinkled mouth
- Lack of connection, little to no physical contact or affection
- Add any others that are not mentioned above

Think of boundaries as property lines around the foundation that you have built thus far through this healing journey. Boundaries are part of your personal soul care. Boundaries enable you to be self-aware of your thoughts, emotions, and actions, which helps you to have empathy and love toward others. Today, society teaches you to shut others out. That is not setting boundaries; it is creating division, which goes against the biblical principle of unity.

Boundaries are also unique and individual to each person, which is why it is important that you set your own boundaries while others set theirs. These are safeguards for both sides. Boundaries are based on your individual values and your self-identity. Therefore, someone else cannot make a boundary for you. This is something you must do for yourself. Remember: don't make boundaries prohibitive, as this will prevent unification as well as undermine where you are trying to go in your relationship with your mother.

1. Identify the specific areas where boundaries need to be set in your relationship with your mother. These boundaries may be emotional, intellectual, or physical, and may be in areas such as time or communication. Feel free to come up with your own categories and types of boundaries based on your needs.
2. Clearly define why you need a particular boundary. Again, you need to understand your why, so that you can set your boundary appropriately.
3. Boundaries are to level set behaviors during your engagements.
4. Boundaries allow you to share your heart in a nonconfrontational way, which over time can break down barriers and open up lines of communication.

Here are a few examples of how I set boundaries with my mother.

Respecting Independence: Both parties should acknowledge each other as independent adults with their own lives, responsibilities, and decisions to make. This means refraining from excessive interference or control in each other's lives.

Early in my career, I would build a job history then move on to the next job working to build my skill set and work experience. My mother believed that I should just find a job and stay there for the rest of my life. For me, her way felt limiting and stifling. Every time I got a new job, instead of celebrating my accomplishment, there would be criticism for changing jobs.

I had to build a boundary with my mother to respect my independence, responsibility, and decision-making around my career. We had differing views, and this was an area in which we would never agree. After setting this boundary, she began to support my decisions in this area and celebrate my success.

Personal Space: Respecting each other's personal space is crucial, whether it is physical space, emotional space, or space for individual pursuits and interests. This includes refraining from showing up unannounced or expecting constant availability.

Remember I told you as a teenager, my personal space was always violated.

As an adult, I set a boundary with my mom that she had to call before showing up at my house. Once she was invited in, she could not go through my personal space looking for anything. After setting this boundary, I could spend time with her in my space without feeling guarded.

Respecting Differences: Acknowledging and respecting each other's differences in opinions, beliefs, and lifestyles is important. It is okay to disagree, but it should be done respectfully, without trying to impose one's views on the other.

As a single mom, I built a close relationship with my son. I allowed him the freedom to discover who he was by giving him more freedom from rules than I had growing up. My mother felt that I was not strict enough with my son and that he needed more rules to follow.

I set a boundary in this area, that she could not impose her views on how he should be raised. She had raised me her way, and I was trying something different. After setting this boundary, my mother kept her opinions to herself about how I was raising my son.

These examples should give you an idea of how to set boundaries with your mother. I have also given you some additional areas to consider that might be applicable to your situation.

Financial Boundaries: Agreeing on financial boundaries helps prevent misunderstandings and conflicts. This may involve decisions about financial support, borrowing money, or sharing expenses in shared endeavors.

Respecting Life Choices: Each party should respect the other's life choices, whether it is career decisions, romantic relationships, or lifestyle choices. Offering support and advice is fine, but ultimately, the final decision should be respected.

Boundaries with Extended Family: Setting boundaries with extended family members, especially regarding interference or criticism from other relatives, can help maintain a healthy mother-daughter relationship.

Time Management: Respect for each other's time is crucial. Both should understand and respect each other's schedules and commitments, avoiding unnecessary demands on each other's time.

Emotional Support versus Emotional Dependency: While it is important to offer emotional support, it is also essential to recognize when boundaries need to be set to prevent emotional dependency or enmeshment.

Self-Care: Encouraging each other to prioritize self-care and well-being is vital. Both should recognize the importance of taking care of themselves physically, emotionally, and mentally, even if it means setting boundaries to ensure this happens.

Clear Communication: Open and honest communication is essential, but so is setting boundaries around what topics are appropriate for discussion and how they are discussed. Both should feel comfortable expressing their needs and preferences without fear of judgment or manipulation.

What to do when communicating your boundaries

- Always use "I" statements not "You" statements. "You" language comes across as accusatory or blaming.
- Always remain calm and breathe. Whenever you feel you might be getting agitated, pause and breathe. The last thing you want to happen is for your emotions to rise up, take over, and start driving the conversation.

What not to do when communicating your boundaries

- Once you have set your boundaries and are ready to communicate them to your mother, do not apologize for setting the boundaries. Often as women, we apologize or give long-winded explanations of our why. This is not empowering behavior.
- If you hear something that bothers you, don't jump to conclusions. Listen and ask clarifying questions.

I have added another supplemental worksheet called "Setting Boundaries" from Therapist Aid, LLC, to the resource section that can be used as practice to work out the conversations you want to have before actually having them.

The task for this section is to work on your boundaries and get clear on them. Or you can do this exercise with your mother as a collaboration and growth exercise for you both. The goal of such an exercise is to come up with agreed-upon boundaries that work for your growing relationship. Remember, you are building a foundation for your future interactions on the solid ground of mutual rules of engagement. This is not an exercise in going back to rehash the past. The past cannot be changed. You are resetting the present for a better, healthier relationship that will be rebuilt over time.

When I reengaged my mother to try for the second time to rebuild our relationship, unlike the first time, I left the exact examples and hurts about the past in the past. I then addressed how those engagements formed and shaped me in my present state. We talked about why I was trying to change and how my old self-perceptions were not serving me in the way I wanted them to, negatively impacting my current relationship with my mother. I stayed in the present, only drawing from the past in terms of how it was being reflected outwardly in the present. This is the same place I want you to be as you work with your mother to rebuild your relationship. This perspective will change the direction of your conversation instantly, as they will see that you are no longer playing the blame game from the past but are trying to grow into the future.

Resolving Conflict, the Healthy Way

The last step in rebuilding your foundation is learning how to manage conflict in a healthy manner. I am no expert in this area, but I did learn to successfully navigate conflict through my many years in the corporate arena, leading teams in large organizations where conflict constantly swirled around, ready to destroy a team and the organization. This experience helped set me up to overcome the unsuccessful conflict management attempt I had made with my mother many years before. The corporate arena taught me conflict resolution and management principles can be used in any relationship engagement.

However, we still need a biblical perspective for this as well. For this, we will look to the master teacher Himself, Jesus. Jesus applied a simple, 3-step method of conflict resolution. 1) stick to the facts, not your emotions; 2) address it immediately, don't wait; 3) forgive and have mercy. These three steps can be difficult to take when we are emotional. For example, instead of responding with facts, we tend to respond emotionally. Where Jesus addresses an issue immediately, we will let it go unaddressed for long periods of time, including forever, which leads us to putting up a defensive wall. Where Jesus extends forgiveness and offers another chance, we tend to allow bitterness to stew and fester, and not give someone another chance.

Jesus has given us the perfect framework for working through conflict in a simple but effective biblical way that supports a better outcome. All you need to do is practice it. You need to stop overcomplicating it. You often avoid it because you are trying to predict what the other party might say or do. Looking through this lens keeps you from doing nothing as a way to avoid discomfort. Remember this whole journey has been about taking steps of courage into uncharted waters. Now is not the time to sit in a boat on the water, bobbing up and down with the tide. It is time to float out into a new part of the water where the waves are calm and peaceful. Emotional intelligence and maturity. . . this is where you are now. Sitting at the table of grace with truth.

The one big thing in conflict resolution and management, besides managing emotion, is communication. In conflict between parties, words are usually driven by emotions with one or both sides trying to be the victor in the situation. Words go back and forth, without either of the two sides reaching an understanding of the needs of the other, or seeking how to get to common ground where both sides feel they are honored and respected with a mutual agreement to forge ahead. This sounds like the same thing that happens in personal relationships too.

Let each one of you look not only to his own interest, but also the interests of others.

—Philippians 2:4, ESV

When you resolve conflict from this biblical perspective, you open yourself to reaching resolutions that work for both parties, not just one side. Again, you are called to be peacemakers and unify your environments. As you have learned, nothing is more important to God than the family unit. If you are walking in the fruit of the spirit, this task should be much easier to accomplish. You cannot be a peacemaker walking out of alignment with grace and a loving heart; it will not work. Being out of alignment always brings strife and opposition.

Here is another supplemental worksheet called Conflict Resolution from Therapist Aid, LLC: www.therapistaid.com/therapy-worksheet/relationship-conflict-resolution to help you during this process. The goal here is to come to a mutually beneficial agreement wherein both of you feel comfortable with your plan of action to maintain respect in your interactions and engagements.

Necessary Resources

Now let me introduce you to two additional resources I want you to use. I like these two books because they are both full of exercises that have already been proven as tools that help build better lines of communication. Effective communication is the tool that is needed to manage conflict. First is the book, *Crucial Conversations,* 3rd Edition by Grenny, et al, (2021). It is a tool that I use constantly, both for myself and with my clients. I use it as a prep tool before I go into a situation where I need my cooler head to prevail. When you prepare for a critical conversation, your confidence is boosted because you have determined your intention and the goals you would like to achieve from the conversation that are mutually beneficial to both parties.

The second book I use personally and with clients is called *The 4 Essential Keys to Effective Communication* by Bento C. Leal III (2017). What I like about this book is the 12-day Communication Challenge. In this challenge, you get to practice becoming a more effective communicator. Practice helps build confidence in your ability to project your thoughts and words with clarity. When you engage from your confident self, you are less likely to get defensive. Again, these resources can be shared so that you and your mother do them together, giving you opportunities to grow and learn together. I am excited at the progress the two of you are already making. I am confident you will be successful in this endeavor.

In the next chapter, I will share with you how putting all this together has healed my own heart, brought my heart and mind into alignment with my authentic self, and reconciled and restored my relationship to a place of honor with my mother. I hope you and your mother are inspired by our story, which is an example of where you and your mother can find yourselves too!

CHAPTER 12

Restoration of Love, Relationship, and Honor

Love is patient and kind; love does not envy or boast; it is not arrogant or rude. It does not insist on its own way; it is not irritable or resentful; it does not rejoice at wrongdoing, but rejoices with the truth. Love bears all things, believes all things, hopes all things, endures all things. Love never ends.

—1 Corinthians 13:4-8, ESV

Since the fall of Adam and Eve, God has been reconciling His people, either back to Himself or within their own environment. He always works on the individual first, setting us up to be successful by building us up in self-love and confidence, which creates the capacity for us to love others. He restores our true, authentic nature, which provides us with strength through Him. He restores us through His everlasting love to transform our souls. Our empowered state gives us wisdom and courage to forge ahead on paths we never saw ourselves taking. These are paths on which we can move forward from our painful past and gain new freedom. This brings us to a peaceful future where we have shed the burden and weight of our past, which have held us down like anchors in our souls. Reconciliation is for everyone. We were put on this earth to love and heal others through love. When there is love, things change.

> Let love be genuine. Abhor what is evil; hold fast to what is good. Love one another with brotherly affection. Outdo one another in showing honor. Do not be slothful in zeal, be fervent in spirit, serve the Lord. Rejoice in hope, be patient in tribulation, be constant in prayer. Contribute to the needs of the saints and seek to show hospitality. (Romans 12:9-13, ESV)

Rewriting Your Future

It is not how you start that matters most, but how you end. I could not be reconnected with my mother until I first looked at how to heal myself. When I started to look at how I could show up in the world and be a peacemaker instead of a negative disruptor, then I could move forward toward reconnection. When I realized that I had the power to repair my own broken fences and bridge gaps within myself, this empowered me to take action to become whole and authentic. Then I could figure out how to mend the fences and bridge the gap with her.

Once I learned and experienced the unbelievable benefits of walking in peace instead of chaos, I could rebuild my own life into one where my mind, heart, and soul would forever be changed. None of this would have been possible without fully surrendering to God and allowing Him to prune me where He knew I was very prickly with thorns on top of thorns. When He pruned me, buds of new life started to form. He took my crackled heart and mended it back together, filling it with love and life. He took me through Romans 12 until I no longer recognized myself as the person I used to be. I gained the gifts of grace outlined in verses 3-8. I started to reflect the "Marks of a True Christian," pouring out love that is genuine and living in harmony and peace with all. I became a better all-round person that I could always be proud of.

Living my life as my authentic self means no longer looking through the lens of not being good enough or what people wanted me to be but through the lens of who I always knew that I was inside. That cool, courageous, funny, take-charge-of-life teenage girl from back in the day with headphones, bell bottoms, and a book had finally come out to play. When I allowed God to heal my fractured and broken pieces, it was as if Jesus had removed the mud with which I had covered my own eyes, blinding myself to the truth. I could see the woman who is my mother with a clear vision of the truth about what had been and what could be for us in the future. I could move to a place that honored her as my mother.

Fortunately, I have been able to figure this out while she is still living. For some of you reading this book, your mother may not be alive anymore. However, you can still reconcile your feelings about her to help you with your healing journey, letting go of the things that cannot be changed in your past, and moving forward with a restored heart of love and gratitude when you think about your mother. Through this journey, God taught me compassion, affection, honor, hope, patience, and love. These were all the things I needed for a reconciliation and restoration of my heart, mind, and soul.

From Then to Now

When I started my own healing journey, my view of my mother moved from judgment to compassion. The blame game I had played for years started to melt away when I took a real interest in getting to know and understand her. What I discovered, to my surprise, was that I had also inherited many of her good parts, along with the unhealthy ones I tried to deny. Prior to this discovery, I had given all the credit for who I was to my father. After all, I looked like him and I followed his every move like a puppy, wanting to grow up and be like him—strong, confident, and commanding in presence. In those teenage years, my father always told me I could be anything I wanted to be. He told me the only limits I had were the ones I placed on myself.

Meanwhile, the conversations my mother had with me always seemed to place limits on what I could or could not do. I felt my father was teaching me independence and my mother was teaching me dependence. My father taught me that I did not need to get married to live a great life, while my mother felt it was important to get married and have a family. Eventually, whatever my father said was what I did. If my mother said something, I did the opposite in an attempt to prove her wrong.

As a teenager, this was very confusing and conflicting. Who was right, my mother or my father? Both. It turns out my parents are two sides of the same coin. Together, they gave me both sides of the equation so that I could be empowered to make the right choices for my life based on all the pertinent information available. My father was raised by a single mother in Louisiana who raised four boys by herself. She had her own business and owned her home, which was unheard of in those days.

My mother was raised in a married environment until her parents divorced. Her views were shaped by the full family experience but as a dysfunctional family, nonetheless. At the end of the day, they wanted what was best for their first-born daughter as well as all their children. They wanted my life to be better than what they experienced growing up in the Jim Crow South. My mother did not want me to fall and be hurt by any of life's circumstances, so she was overly cautious and protective, which caused friction in our relationship. I was trying to prove to her that I was responsible, begging for her to give me some rope to move around and discover life for myself, while she was trying to keep me close to avoid any traps or pitfalls that I did not know existed. In the end, the rope that was supposed to be my lifeline to her became the rope that nearly strangled our relationship to death.

Beauty Found in Reconnection

Today, that rope has turned into a three-strand cord with God, my mother, and me, joined together continually and discovering our new relationship as mother and daughter. We talk on the phone weekly. If I don't call her within a couple of days, she will call me to see what is going on. We laugh and catch up on what is going on in each other's worlds, her with her jewelry-making and me with all my various projects.

We talk about my granddaughter, who my mom has always said has mannerisms and a physical appearance just like mine. I believe we both look at my granddaughter as a new opportunity to share her spirit in ways we lost many years ago. When we are in the same space, she watches me and I watch her, she listens to me, and I listen to her. We hug, embrace, and say "I love you."

We have conversations about dreams past and present. I am constantly learning new things about my mother I didn't know before, which is super cool. I often think about the good things I got from my mother, like my ability to question everything and really examine things that do not seem quite right. I got my love of shoes, clothes, and make-up from my mother. She has always been a fashionista. For many years, she made all of our clothes and taught my sister and me to sew as well. I no longer sew because I hate it and prefer to wear clothes off the rack. There is an Easter picture of my mother, my sister, and me when I was about four years old. She made us all matching white dresses for Easter Sunday. My sister and I had white shoes with our dresses, but my mother popped her dress off with candy apple red patent leather stilettos with a matching purse. I have been on the hunt for my own candy apple red stilettos my entire life since the age of four. I do have a solid shoe game because of my mother. This Easter photo is my favorite picture of all time.

My mother is sassy and, according to her siblings, this has been the case all her life. She is very much an extrovert and will talk to anyone and everyone within earshot. My mother has a big personality that I have always admired. You know when she enters a room full of people. You will see her first in an outfit that will make you say "Wow," and then you will hear her. Her personality is the opposite of mine. I prefer to be at home, curled up with a book or watching a movie in sweats, a T-shirt, and fuzzy slippers.

You might see me when I enter a room because I am a six-foot-tall woman who likes to wear high heels, making me even taller, but you will never hear me in a room unless I am speaking to the room for some specific reason. My mother is very witty and funny. I know for sure

I got that gift from her. She has always been the voice of optimism. When I rediscovered her, I actually became more optimistic in life.

Remember I said that, whatever my mother did, I did the opposite, so I became a pessimist. Again, she was so right. It is much better to live life through the eyes of optimism rather than pessimism. I'm amazed at the years I spent looking at the glass as half empty. My mother is at her heart a nurturer of her family. She is like a momma bear, always protecting her bear cubs, even in adulthood. I try to remind her that her children are all grown and that she is no longer obligated to be the protective mother, so she can relax and not worry so much. Today I am seeking to grow in friendship with her. She is old school, which means she will always mother us, whether we need it to or not.

Our Relationship Today

My mother and I have come a long way in our relationship. We have come to a place I never imagined—a reconciled place of peace and joy. I often wonder if this would have ever happened had I not taken steps to repair our relationship. My mother can hold a grudge until the end of time. I too used to be able to do that, but since God worked on me in this area, I prefer to mend fences and build bridges of hope in relationships instead of staying disconnected forever.

Does my mother say things from time to time that strike that nerve? Yes. Depending on what it is, I will address it or let it go, and this is the difference between where we used to be and where we are today. I did not ask her to change; I changed. In the evolution of our growing relationship, we both changed. I like to think we both healed some of the fractured places inside of us, together. These places are not all healed, but we are well on our way. We are not fully restored until we get to heaven, but where are today feels like we are closer to total healing than not.

I believe once she reads this book in its entirety, there will be some additional healing for her too in those places I know nothing about that are only private to her and her life experience. Growing up, she was the teacher, and I was the student. Today, the tables have turned in some areas where I am the teacher, and she is the student. We all have the power to change who we are, but it requires work, honesty, and choice. Not everyone, including our mothers, will be willing to do what is necessary to become something different.

I have often heard my mother say she likes herself just the way she is. She freely admits that in my teenage years she might have been a little overprotective. Whether or not she changes is her choice. I have chosen how I want to live my life with her in it. I am not looking for the storybook version of what I once wanted from her; I am looking for the version of our relationship that works for both of us today.

I cannot change what happened all those years ago between us. I can never unwrite the B-word I wrote years ago, but I can repent to God and to her, then move forward in the earnest belief that our future will be different from our past. I believe those of you reading this book can have the mother-daughter relationship your heart has been crying for all these years. Will it look different? Yes. The beauty of it is this: would you rather rebuild that relationship with her while she is still here or think about what you could have done after she is gone? Today, I constantly hear the words "I love you" from my mom more than I ever thought was possible. She is constantly telling me how proud she is of me for everything I do. As a teenager, I would have given up pepperoni pizza, cheeseburgers, and French fries to hear her say those words to me.

Back then, in my immaturity, I might not have appreciated those words as much as I do now. They are a gift to my soul. There is no feeling in the world like the realization that your mother genuinely loves who you are. Discovering this allows us to go back and reconcile the mind and heart of our younger selves to let go of the past and allow the future to be shaped by the present. We are not the same people we were, and neither are our mothers. Time has molded and shaped our thoughts, our dreams, and our hopes for the future. To get to these reshaped futures, we will need compassion, patience, hope, and empathy with open hearts and minds.

My story with my mother did not end in sadness or regret. It began again in hope, sprinkled with some fear that turned into love bringing us back to full reconciliation and restoration as a mother-daughter unit. It was like the story of the Prodigal Son in the Bible I spoke about earlier. When the son finally realized he had made a huge mistake by trying to live his life separated from a key relationship, he returned to his father. When I began to realize that my severed relationship with my mother was at the core of most of my life challenges, I began to figure out how to come back to the most critical relationship that I have —the giver of my natural life, my mother. When I decided to work to restore honor to my mother in my life, God began to help me figure it out. I did not come back with my head hanging low; I came back as a confident daughter, acknowledging the importance of my mother to and in my life.

I am sharing our story at this point in this book because I want you to see what is possible for you. I have a lot of hope and belief that many more mothers and daughters will find their way back to each other, restoring their relationships with love, laughter, respect, and admiration, changing the trajectory of their families for future generations. My prayer for each and every one of you reading this book is to find exactly what you need to get your relationships healed and whole as mothers and daughters, bringing honor to God through your powerful process of reconciliation and restoration.

Congratulations on being so courageous and successful on this journey thus far. You have made incredible progress healing your soul and forging your new relationship with your mother with new tools to help you both navigate your new relationship together. You both are crafting a beautiful new relationship built on mutual respect, trust, and love. That is truly amazing! I know God is looking down and smiling at all the restored mothers and daughters. May all be well in your souls!

Restoration Blueprint Exercise

Now that you have learned my "Where Are We Now" story, I want you to start to memorialize your own "Where Are They Now" story with your mother as it stands today. This is the last exercise in your Restoration Blueprint, so take out your journal or companion guide to capture this information.

Hopefully, by this juncture, you have had some real, meaningful interactions and engagements with your mother on your path of restoration. I have listed a few of the questions from earlier in the book and added some additional ones for you to start to gauge where your relationship is today with your mother. This Restoration Blueprint Exercise is intended to track your progress in the growth and development of your new relationship.

- What did you hope to gain from the restored relationship?
- What does your relationship look like today?
- How have you changed because you are reconnected in a healthy way with your mother?
- What, if any, changes can you see in your mother?

- What do you appreciate about your mother now that you did not before?
- What did you learn about her through this process that surprised you?
- Name three things you now appreciate about her that you didn't before.
- Name three positive attributes you possess that you got from your mother.
- How do you feel about your relationship today versus where you were when you started this book?

A Prayer of Restoration and Love

Dear Heavenly Father,

Thank You for being with us throughout this journey toward reconciliation with our mothers.

When we first started, we were filled with anxiety, trepidation, and fear of this unknown path.

We clung onto the promise that You would never leave us or forsake us, and You did not.

From our mending hearts, we give You gratitude and appreciation that Your ways are always higher than our ways, and that Your thoughts are greater than our thoughts will ever be.

When we were in the place of unbelief that we could ever rebuild a relationship with our mothers, You walked us through step by step, helping us build the path that led to reconciliation, restoring our brokenness to wholeness throughout the journey.

Today, we are in a place we could not see with our own eyes, but that you clearly saw for us—in a loving relationship once again with our mothers.

Your awesome and powerful love helped us move to a place of acceptance and forgiveness we did not think was possible, reminding us once again that all things are possible with You.

Thank you for teaching us this powerful lesson of restoration, reconciliation, and love.

We now see with open eyes that our life experiences were our stepping stones on the path of discovery of ourselves through Your tender grace and mercy.

This path showed us that in You we can find our healing, which will lead us to joy and peace.

As we continue to move forward in love, we thank You in advance for the continued healing we will receive.

We thank You for helping us to let go of the past and look forward with hope for the future.

We thank You for allowing us to accept that our mothers are not perfect and that we can let go of the judgment we have held onto and directed toward them.

We thank You, Lord, that You have brought us to this place of growth where we can learn to love ourselves, let go of our past mistakes, and grow in maturity for a brighter future.

We acknowledge as we have worked to restore our mothers to a place of honor, that we have also given You the honor and glory that is due You.

In the blessed name of Jesus Christ. Amen!

CHAPTER 13

Restoration Blueprint for Honor and Love

"Honor your father and mother"—which is the first commandment with a promise—so that it may go well with you and that you may enjoy long life on the earth.

—Ephesians 6:2-3, NIV

When you began this book, the call to action was to learn how to honor God's command to honor your mother. As we see in Ephesians 6:2, this command ends with a promise from God. I don't know what your exact fulfilled promise will be but as you can see above, God's promise is clear in verse 3. In His time, He will reveal the promise to you for bringing honor to your mother which also brings honor to Him.

As you went through the three-part journey allowing God to Reveal, Jesus to Reconstruct, and the Holy Spirit to Transform your thoughts, beliefs, emotions, and actions, you took major steps on your HEALING journey. Hopefully, you have already begun to experience some breakthroughs personally and with your mother as you have gone through each chapter. Let's summarize the entire journey so that you can see the full Restoration Blueprint laid out to show what is achievable for you and your relationship with your mother.

Part 1—Journey to Reveal
Journey of Discovery

You covered God's principles regarding mothers and why this critical relationship was created. You set up the first context for you to view the mother-daughter relationship and its value to you, the daughter. You also acknowledged the challenges this complex relationship has in how it shapes how you view yourself when it has not been healthy. Throughout the book, you covered some very emotional ground to set you up to have "aha" moments and breakthroughs during your healing journey.

The first step you took to start the healing process was to sit in meditation and visualize a younger version of yourself, showing appreciation for the efforts you previously put forth trying to make a connection to your mother and reconcile your feelings of hurt, guilt, shame, or disappointment as you longed for the experience with your mother that eluded you. This was done to start the process of releasing emotions attached to the past. Your bravery in doing this exercise hopefully brought you to a place deep inside that you had forgotten about. There, you saw the possibility that you could rise up and break free from the past because you found your center of courage. You did this by discovering that it has always been inside of you but was only covered up by life experiences.

You tackled some hard steps as you journeyed through another centering exercise to start to feel and imagine what a healed soul would feel like with a heart of gratitude in appreciation for the new journey. You bravely looked at your past experiences and analyzed them as you started to build your Restoration Blueprint through journaling about your relationship with your mother from a look back. In this exercise, you revealed how your relationship was with your mother from your younger perspective. You took a hard look at how this has manifested in your thoughts and feelings about yourself and the impact of this jaded view. You looked at how this has impacted other relationships in your life. You described where your current relationship was with your mother at the start of this book. Lastly, you envisioned or dreamed where you wanted this relationship to be in your future.

You discovered the value and importance of exploring the truth instead of living in the stories you might have believed about your past that may have skewed the truth. You acknowledged where you had been through truth statements. Then you created truth and value statements for yourself that are personal to you so that you could speak them aloud to hear your own voice speaking truth to yourself. In doing this, you should have been able to release some negative emotions you believed about yourself and start to engage with and believe what is actually true about you—that you are "fearfully and wonderfully made." (Psalm 139:14, ESV) Since you are a product of our Creator, what better way to start these statements than with "I am."

You learned to accept and let go of past experiences with your mother. This was key because when you dwell on the past, you become stuck in the world of what might have been or what was instead of a forward look at what a new possibility could bring. The pivotal keys in this chapter were learning to extend continuous grace and build compassion, leading to forgiveness of yourself and of your mother. The exercises helped close the eyes of judgment and open your eyes of love with a new perspective. You learned to clear space for your mind to become open through meditation and prayer, which also releases fear and anxiety as you learn new information. You also learned to process your emotions in a healthy way, which benefits you by connecting your heart and head in the same good space. You added your truth and value statements to further solidify your heart's desire to grow in love.

Part 2—Journey to Reconstruct
Building a Good Foundation

Part 2 of this book was all about having personal breakthroughs to help you move forward and build a new foundation for yourself based on truth. When you can have breakthroughs, whether they are in your mind or your heart, you mentally and physically expand your confidence and belief in the idea that change is possible. Exploring emotions, thoughts, and belief systems that were developed from a place of discontent revealed stories and emotions that were not necessarily reality or truth. This enabled you to view your current and future state from a new perspective through the eyes and emotions of encouragement and positivity. This perspective allowed you to release and let go of your past experiences. These exercises were created to empower you and propel you forward so you could rebuild a solid foundation as you start to reengage and build your future relationship with your mother.

I pray and hope you learned the value of true forgiveness in Part 2. Forgiveness is an area most people never master. It is difficult for many reasons, but it would not be a cornerstone in Christianity or in life for that matter if it were not vitality important for us to learn to do. There are so many benefits to learning to forgive—mentally, physically, and of course spiritually. If more people could practice true forgiveness, there would be more love and less conflict in the world. As I said earlier, it takes constant practice to extend forgiveness with grace and love. These are skills you will be practicing for the rest of your life. The more you practice, the easier they get.

True practice shows up when something happens that tests your human capacity to deal with adversity. Remember, you are not a perfect being, and there will be times when you will not practice grace or forgiveness as you should. The key will be to continue moving forward and not beat yourself up in these instances. Remember that they are only temporary moments in the grand scheme of life. The forgiveness exercises you learned can be used each time you are faced with a situation that requires your forgiveness.

From this section, your toolkit now contains new tools because you took a deep dive into how your emotions were really driving your actions in all the relationship areas of your life. You focused primarily on the mindset. This is because where your mind is your actions generally follow. You learned how to navigate and use emotional intelligence. You mapped out how you would like to see yourself show up in the world every day with your new mindset. In doing so, you can bring peace to your environment instead of disruption. When you can break free of old patterns, you can start to embody what is on the inside—God's nature of love and civility, which leads you to unity and reconnection.

In this section, you also learned to accept responsibility and accountability. These are key because this shows that no one can lead you to a place that you do not want to go. As a result, you are not blaming others for your thoughts, actions, or experiences because you know you have control in all of those areas in any situation. You learned to stay in your own lane and change what you are responsible for. Remember, it's your life you are navigating, I want you to do so from a healed and empowered state.

The most powerful assignment of this book was writing a love letter to your mother. In doing so, you got to display acceptance, forgiveness, grace, and love with your desire for reconciliation and future growth in your relationship with your mother. You took the opportunity to show her what a strong and resilient daughter you have become. You allowed her to have a peek into your past, not to blame but to show her the impact of the past. Then you shared your heart's desire to reconnect with her differently, to build a new and better relationship for the two of you and the future of your family. You also discussed the benefits your restored relationship will bring to your family for generations to come. You should be very proud of yourself for completing this assignment and then spending time with your mother, using it as a reconnection point in your relationship.

In this section, you also looked back into your family history to break down generational patterns. You also enlisted your mother's help in this area, further moving toward building a working relationship with her to heal the future of your family. You started to understand barriers and patterns within your family that have left many wounded souls. In this section, you obtained and used tools that will help facilitate healthier relationships with your family, which will lead to stronger bonds and family ties, both now and in the future. This work is healing the hearts and souls of your family more than you will ever know. As Psalm 147:3 (ESV) reminds us, "He heals the brokenhearted and binds up their wounds." As you do your part, God will most certainly be doing His part as the greatest Healer of all.

Part 3—Journey to Transform
Transformation of the Heart & Soul

The transformative work you did in Part 3 was a three-part journey. In this section, your life's journey is about facilitating God's love from your authentic self. The journey is also about expanding God's love as you walk through life, encountering people along the way. Our goal as Christians is to expand the Kingdom of God here on Earth. How do we do this? By consistently showing love to everyone we encounter from the path we have already walked. Walking this path from a healed and restored position gives you not only confidence but also the stories to tell others as proof of what is possible for everyone. You get to show them that everything starts with us first and then expands outward to others. Your story of reconciliation and reconnection with your mother becomes center-stage because the most difficult relationship in your life now has purpose and meaning behind it, and it shines a bright light on the power of redemption.

I pray that as you continue to explore and rebuild your relationship with your mother, you will continue to blossom and grow into a beautiful mother-daughter unit. I pray your healing journey continues and that, as you look at your family from generations past, you also find out some magnificent and wonderful things about your family. Allow these new findings to empower you to continue this healing and restorative journey for your family. Often, when you look back into the past, your view has been clouded by your experiences or the experiences of others. Looking into the past with a fresh, new perspective should open your heart and mind to see some of the beautiful parts of your family that may have been obscured by the lens of negative experiences. Getting beyond the secrets, lies, and hurtful spots may also need to happen collectively for your family, but you now have a framework and tools to help facilitate this path for your family. You know the benefits healing and transformation can bring. You also have learned some new skills and tools needed to break through those old, learned behaviors so you will be able to help others along the way. Remember as you continue to do this work that your original intention was to rebuild your relationship with your mother and allow that to drive your actions.

You learned some valuable tools that helped you build respect and boundaries and manage conflict appropriately. These elements are key to success as you navigate your healed relationship. Remember that great communication is also key in relationship-building. Your words have the power to build up or tear down not only yourself but others too. You know the power of words firsthand, so choose words that empower and build as you communicate these key areas. Spread your seeds of love through empowering words and actions as you walk your life journey. Scripture teaches us, "One gives freely, yet grows all the richer; another withholds what he should give, and only suffers want. Whoever brings blessing will be enriched, and one who waters will himself be watered." (Proverbs 11:24-25, ESV)

CHAPTER 14

The Transformative Power of Reconciliation

Above all, keep loving one another earnestly, since love covers a multitude of sins.

— 1 Peter 4:8, ESV

Hello, Daughters!

You have made it! Congratulations. I am so proud of you for hanging in there and completing the book and all the exercises contained within. In the beginning, before you stepped onto the path for this complicated journey, you could not envision what rebuilding a relationship with your mother could look like because you did not have the tools or knowledge to rebuild a relationship with your mother. Now you possess not only the knowledge but tools to help you make this dream a reality. You have already taken the first steps with your mother and are working together to rebuild your mother-daughter relationship. That is amazing!

You should be very proud of yourself for the soul-healing work that you did. You got angry, you cried, you persevered and most importantly you never gave up on yourself or on having a relationship with your mother. You learned to look at her and love her in a new context through the eyes of love and appreciation for the gift of life. Love is the greatest commandment Jesus gives us. As 1 Peter 4:8 teaches us, love changes our perspective and leads us down a path of forgiveness, grace, and mercy.

As ministers of reconciliation within our environments, you are charged with creating and fostering peaceful, healthy environments to elevate people around you with growth and care as God's children. Reconnecting with your mother is a powerful example of reconciliation. You are now equipped to continue this journey both for now and in the future. God has seen all of your efforts through this journey. Nothing has been missed by Him. Matthew 5:9 (NLT) gives us another promise from Him. "God blesses those who work for peace, for they will be called the children of God." Nothing pleases God more than to see family ties mended and thriving for generations to come, living in peace. Again, be proud of the tremendous work you did, it not only benefits you, but it also benefits your entire family for generations to come. This is the greatest gift of them all.

As this book ends, remember where you started and the path you took to where you have come to now. You took a very hard journey to Reveal, Reconstruct, and Transform not only your relationship with your mother but also yourself. You are not the same person you were when you began this journey. Your heart and mind are now in alignment with your authentic self. You are showing up more confidently and powerfully in the world. You are using your new and practical tools through daily practice, and you are continuing to move forward toward a brighter future each day. Often as women, we do not give ourselves credit for the progress we make, so take the time to celebrate this great accomplishment of forward progress. You earned this celebration!

Your Restoration Blueprint toolkit now contains tools to help you continue to Reveal any other areas in your relationship with your mother that still need healing, as well as other areas of life that may not be serving you in the way you want, like relationships with your significant others, children, siblings, and even your fathers. These tools are universal and have been designed to be used again and again. In the Reveal stage, you walked those Hard Steps to identify emotions connected to the relationship you are working to rebuild. Know that you must always Explore the Truth so that you can process thoughts and emotions appropriately, replacing the untruth with the truth, releasing those old stories in your head. Then you can finally Accept the Past and leave those emotions and stories in the past where they belong, while you look toward a brighter future.

You also have new tools to Reconstruct the new relationship. In the reconstruction phase, you learned to Let It Go through real forgiveness of yourself and your mother. You now have a better understanding of the benefits of forgiveness in your mental, physical, and spiritual state. You have journaled to release thoughts and emotions and also meditated to get grounded and centered for real change. Through this process you have learned to Ignite Self-Love, always ensuring that you are doing things to build up your self-esteem, also through forgiveness. You took charge to Navigate Your Healing Relationship by beautifully crafting a love letter to your mother and taking her on a date to reconnect your soul with hers through this letter. You facilitated opening the door to new possibilities with your mother beyond both of your wildest expectations. You also enlisted your mother to tackle familial patterns that have followed your family for generations and create new Generational Overrides to break through those old wounds. You both did some work to unmask the secrets and patterns that have caused destructive areas within your family, holding them back for generations. You are working to build a stronger future for your family for generations to come. Nice job, ladies!

You have now experienced the power of transformational reconciliation and the gifts it brings to your life. You are empowered to Transform relationships with tangible tools that build respect and healthy boundaries and resolve conflict for positive outcomes. You are set on your new course for a continual transformational experience for years to come. You can now continue growing and developing with and through love of self and love toward others, making your presence bigger and brighter out in the world. As you become who you want and were meant to become, live authentically, reach your highest potential, and transform your life!

Afterword

Putting Your Restoration Blueprint into Action

At the beginning of this book, I committed to show you through the processes and exercises in this book that you would be able to . . .

- Accept and let go of the past
- Forgive and open your heart
- Heal and move forward in more love for self and others
- Live authentically and impactfully
- Honor and love your mother in a new relationship
- Build stronger generations to come

Now the time has come for you to continue to put your Restoration Blueprint into everyday actions and activities. Just because this book is closing does not mean you get to close the book and walk away. This is a lifetime journey that needs to continue to unfold day by day, month after month, year after year for generations to come.

I also committed to walk with you on this path. Are you ready to dive deeper into these concepts and work directly with me? If so, go to my website and set up a discovery session call at www. chequitamccullough.com. I look forward to getting to know more about you and walking with you even more deeply on your journey of reconciliation and reconnection with your mother. Don't hesitate.

You have already made great progress. I want to continue to support you where you are today and help you live powerfully with authenticity, confidence, and empowerment.

Acknowledgments

To my cousin, Whitney, who inspired this book. We are two cousins working together in the quest to have positive, loving relationships with our mothers, and make a powerful impact in the lives of our families. Love you, girl!

To my sister, Rita, my biggest fan and cheerleader for all her life. Thank you, little sis, for always supporting me. I know you had to walk behind my big shoes which was not always easy. I love you!

To my brother, J.R., who came into the picture during my turbulent teenage years. Thank you for always looking up at me with little-brother eyes of love. Those eyes helped me become a better person. I love you!

To my son, Ryan, thank you for always making me feel like your hero even when I was still trying to figure out who I was. You are an amazing man, who has loved me unconditionally all your life. I love you!

To my granddaughter Zoey, most people call you a mini version of me. You inspire me to be fearless, funny, and the best Lola on the planet. I love you!

To the rest of my family, thank you all for supporting me on this book journey as well as in life. Your ideas and encouragement helped to fuel me to the finish line. I love you all!

To all my friends, thank you for your years of support. It is good to know I have strong shoulders to cry on and words of encouragement to lift me up in life. I love you all!

To all the daughters who read this book, my prayer is that your souls will be healed and that you will flourish in reconciliation, restoration, and much love with your mothers!

References and Resources

Bible Gateway. https://www.biblegateway.com/

Bucher, Meg. 2021."'Honor Your Father and Mother': A Biblical Command We Never Outgrow." *Bible Study Tools.* April 28. https://www.biblestudytools.com/bible-study/topical-studies/a-biblical-command-we-never-outgrow-honor-your-father-and-mother.html

"clamor." *The Oxford Pocket Dictionary of Current English.* Encyclopedia.com. (February 7, 2024). https://www.encyclopedia.com/humanities/dictionaries-thesauruses-pictures-and-press-releases/clamor-0

Erb, Bre. 2022. "Restored by God's Love." Previously Unpublished, November, 2022.

Grand, David. 2017. "What Is Brainspotting?" *Brainspotting.* https://brainspotting.com/about-bsp/what-is-brainspotting/

Grenny, Joseph, et al. 2021. *Crucial Conversations: Tools for Talking When Stakes Are High, Third Edition.* New York: McGraw Hill.

Leal, Bento C. III. 2017. *4 Essential Keys to Effective Communication.* CreateSpace Independent Publishing Platform, 2017.

Johns Hopkins Medicine. 2024. "Forgiveness: Your Health Depends on It." *Johns Hopkins Medicine.* https://www.hopkinsmedicine. org/health/wellness-and-prevention/forgiveness-your-health-depends-on-it, Accessed February 11, 2024.

Therapist Aid, LLC. 2017. "Four Phases of Forgiveness." *Therapist Aid.* https://www.therapistaid.com/therapy-worksheet/forgiveness-therapy

Therapist Aid, LLC. 2013. "Relationship Conflict Resolution." *Therapist Aid.* https://www.therapistaid.com/therapy-worksheet/relationship-conflict-resolution.

Therapist Aid, LLC. 2019. "Setting Boundaries." *Therapist Aid.* https://www.therapistaid.com/therapy-worksheet/setting-boundaries

About the Author

Chequita McCullough is a corporate leader and trainer, a minister, speaker, adjunct professor, professional mentor, and transformational coach. She is committed to a relentless pursuit of leading women to become empowered and reach their highest potential, using their voices to change their personal environments.

Born in Louisiana but raised as an "Army brat" traveling the world, she landed in Monterey, CA, as a young girl, where she lived out her experiences detailed in this book. Her experiences drove her to figure out what the mother-daughter relationship could be.

She pursued a career in the corporate world, working for over twenty years in commercial real estate, where she rose up quickly as a leader among leaders. In this career, she often transformed her workplace into a better environment through collaboration, teamwork, and unity. This is also where she cultivated her drive for diversity, equity, and inclusivity for all. Later in her career, she completed her undergraduate degree in leadership and ministry and a master's degree in organizational leadership, both from Grace Christian University.

Her approach to life is simple: being a "doer of the Word" (James 1:22) and reflecting what Jesus taught, bringing Heaven to Earth by demonstrating love, compassion, inspiration, and empowerment for those she meets on her life journey.

Chequita resides in the Hampton Roads area of Virginia, and is a dedicated mother to one adult son, and grandmother to a precious granddaughter.

Chequita McCullough